MW00324128

"The Magicial Language o[
and benefited from reading. ~~Runes have yet to be utilized~~
and accepted on the scale of the tarot, I-Ching, and astrology; if any book can change that, it is P.M.H. Atwater's. In
this book we walk with her as beginners. We are introduced
to the runes, and become familiar with their Celtic roots
and history. She explicitly and comfortably explains the use
of runes in a poetic, spiritual fashion, and provides superb,
in-depth examples of interpretations of castings. When she
is through we feel as if we have gotten to know the runes not
only as a new set of tools, but also as a new friend. After
reading *The Magical Language of Runes* I feel that I can and
will use them easily and often to enhance my understanding
of life."

Michael Peter Langevin
co-publisher of Magical Blend *magazine*

"As old as Odin, as new as the user's inner voice, the runes
speak 'the unspoken language' of intuition and insight.
P.M.H. Atwater's approach is *experiential*, rather than didac-
tic, and teaches the reader to listen for the 'magical language' of the runes as spiritual friends, not merely as divinatory devices."

E. Otha Wingo Ph.D.,
author; director of Huna Research, Inc.

"P.M.H. Atwater introduced me to the runes in 1983. I was
deeply impressed with her skill and the reverence she
brought to this ancient art of divination. In writing this
book, Phyllis makes her considerable ability available to
others. I highly recommend this work."

Carolyn M. Myss
author of The Creation of Health

"I'm thrilled to have *The Magical Language of Runes* in the Wise Woman Center's Green Witch and Goddess Library. The Wise Woman Way—of knowing from within—of remembering, rather than acquiring wisdom—is vividly and delightfully brought to the art of rune casting in this book. P.M.H. Atwater shares secrets seasoned by experience, ideas clearly drawn out, and memories, a deep and sure sense of the way of the ancient wise ones."

Susun S. Weed
founder of the Wise Woman Center
author of Wise Woman Herbal *series.*

"*The Magical Language of Runes* brings a practical, down-to-earth approach to the ancient practice of divination, using our brothers and sisters of the mineral kingdom. Phyllis Atwater brings her own experience and her lyrical use of the English language to a subject often made too complicated for a true and deep understanding. I wholeheartedly recommend this book to anyone interested in increasing their understanding of life."

Wabun Wind
author of Woman of the Dawn
co-author with Sun Bear of The Medicine Wheel: Earth Astrology

"P.M.H. Atwater is a wonderfully talented lady, and this time she has created a delightful book of the magic of runes. Her research into this subject is very significant work. A must read!"

Bryce Bond
host/producer of
TV's "Dimensions in Parapsychology," New York City

"P.M.H. Atwater has the magical capacity to reach and touch the reader through her words, allowing them a direct experience of her. She speaks directly and simply to the reader's experience, creating a context for easy learning, practice and the development of intuition. With this book, the reader travels effortlessly from tuition to intuition, from the external teachers to the internal teacher. . . . Her philosophy is obviously a new paradigm, for a new age, and a new people. At once exciting, and convincing, it becomes our philosophy, too. From this philosophic foundation, we can begin to grow and expand our power and our individuality. I cannot praise this book too highly, for it is really a modern masterpiece among the plethora of new age 'self-help' books."

Enid Hoffman
author of Huna: A Beginner's Guide

"In this most accessible work, P.M.H. Atwater describes how the ancient and powerful divinatory sigils called runes came to her at a point of spiritual crisis in her life and how she learned to work with them and understand them on many levels on which they operate. While factually informative, hers is a human account of the subject rather than an austere, scholarly analysis. She touches on many crucial aspects of the divinatory process."

Paul Devereux
author; editor of The Ley Hunter
director of The Dragon Project Trust

The Magical Language of
RUNES

The Magical Language of
RUNES

P.M.H. Atwater

BEAR & COMPANY
PUBLISHING
SANTA FE, NEW MEXICO

Library of Congress Cataloging-in-Publication Data

Atwater, P.M.H.
    The magical languages of runes / P.M.H. Atwater.
        p.   cm.
    Includes bibliographical references.
    ISBN 0-939680-70-X
    1. Fortune-telling by runes.   I. Title.
    BF1891.R85A78   1990
    133.3'3—dc20   89-39281
                                                           CIP

Copyright © 1986, 1990 by P.M.H. Atwater

All rights reserved. No part of this book may be reproduced by any means and in any form whatsoever without written permission from the publisher, except for brief quotations embodied in literary articles or reviews.

Bear & Company
Santa Fe, NM 87504-2860

Cover, interior design, and wash illustrations: Kathleen Katz
Cover photograph: Anthony F. Holmes
Charts and historical representations: P.M.H. Atwater
Renderings of P.M.H. Atwater's diagrams: Kathleen Katz
Editing: Gail Vivino
Typography: Casa Sin Nombre
Printed in the United States of America by R.R. Donnelley

9 8 7 6 5 4 3 2 1

chapters within

My sincere thanks to Dennis Lee Swartz for the inspiration to write this book, and to Patricia Helen Horne for the kind of guidance and support which makes all things possible.

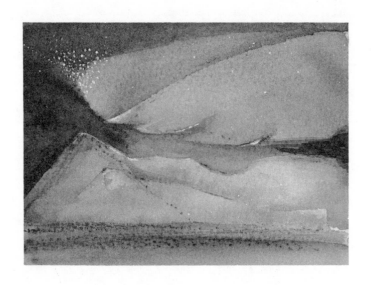

introduction

It was an evening meeting at a friend's house. Many people were packed in the large living room: some sprawled across the floor, others seated in a variety of chairs or standing. The meeting was a "welcome-to-Boise-Idaho" party for a troupe who had just moved to town from California. None of us knew any of them, but the evening's host explained how he had perchanced news of their arrival and felt it only proper to extend a true western welcome with a gathering such as this. We had come to say "hello."

Introductions revealed that the new people were a colorful lot, all well-versed in theatre, arts and crafts, Renaissance history, and Celtic lore. As a way of expressing gratitude for our jovial welcome, one woman in the troupe said she practiced casting runes and, with our permission, would demonstrate what runes were and how they worked. None of us knew anything about runes so we all readily agreed to what seemed like a new form of entertainment.

The woman sat upon the floor and produced from a velvet pouch a handful of small, soft-black pebbles, each graven with a strange, sharp-angled glyph. She invited several people to ask questions of the stones, and said she would seek for answers by casting them. I don't remember much of what came next nor much about any words which were spoken, but I do remember clearly the awe I felt as stones flew from her hands with each cast. In falling, they formed the most fascinating patterns — patterns which sprang to life for me in multidimensional textures, sounds, and smells, as if they possessed the vitality of pulse and breath. I was spellbound.

The woman's voice rambled past my awareness as I concentrated silently on each cast in the privacy of my own mind, interpreting for myself the meanings, correcting what seemed to be her mistakes, and adding additional information. When the woman finished with the demonstration, she turned abruptly in my direction and stated out loud, "You can read these runes better than I." Before I knew what was happening or why, I heard myself reply, "You are correct. I can."

While other people expressed excitement about the strange runes, I quietly pondered what had just happened. I had never before seen anything quite like runes and consciously knew nothing of their history or usage, yet suddenly I knew all about them. This puzzled me.

Later, after almost everyone had left, I was finally able to speak with the woman privately. When I asked why she had said what she did, her answer only added to my puzzle: "I knew you knew." There was a mysterious smile on her lips when she said that, and I found myself requesting a pouch of stones like hers before I had a chance to think. "For fifteen dollars I'll make you a set," she said, and then went on to explain what kind of stones worked best and how each would be selected. "You're getting a bargain, you know, for I spend as much as an hour meditating on each pebble to make certain both glyph and stone fit each other perfectly. The pouch is all hand-sewn." I accepted.

Several weeks went by when, on the night of the full moon as a large group of us gathered for prayer and meditation, she appeared and presented me with the finished pouch of pebbles. I paid her, but felt strongly within myself not to open the pouch, that it must first be blest and "cleansed" during meditation, and then laid to rest until some date in the unknown future which awaited me.

Using the evening's enhanced energies, I enclosed the pouch within my cupped hands and, in my mind's eye, envisioned beams and splashes of radiant light and pure love filling and cleansing the new bundle. In prayer, I asked for divine guidance to know how and when to use runes, and then I dedicated them to God's holy will. The pouch grew hot and tingled as if an electric current had passed through it. Afterwards, I gently placed the rune pouch in my purse and spoke no more of the event.

A week later I left Boise, Idaho, literally closing the door on a lifetime of living, and leaving behind everything and everyone I had ever known. This was August of 1978.

A year and a half before, I had physically died three times and had revived after each episode. I was now newly healed. During those death events, I had experienced the phenomenon known as the near-death experience; that is to say, I had crossed over to The Other Side. Each episode had been different, yet each one had somehow led into the next as if they were progressive. These episodes had affected me so radically that earth life had lost all relevance. For this reason, it had become necessary for me to relearn every aspect of life on every level. In doing this, I had discovered myself to be different. Somehow I had expanded. I was more of me.

In this newness which I had become, I sold a house I had just purchased, I gave away, sold, or stored everything I owned, and I quit an excellent job the very day a major promotion and raise were offered. What seemed needed for survival I stuffed into my little Ford Pinto, then I embarked upon a spiritual odyssey which led first to the Shanti Nilaya Center of Elisabeth Kübler-Ross, at that time located near Escondido, California, where I shared with others the depths of death and the heights of life everlasting. From there, I zigzagged across the entire continent, leaving behind the Pacific's silver sunsets and finding to my delight that sunrises over the Atlantic are indeed drenched with gold.

It was during this odyssey, near the yawning chasms of the Grand Canyon, that I opened the rune pouch for the first time and spilled across my lap the strange stones, all sixteen of them, complete with brief instructions for their use. I felt myself to be a child again, holding my new toys. From that moment on I played with them daily, experimenting, studying every possible variation and nuance of question and throw. Sometimes I would involve others in my play, even groups of others, as I probed ever deeper, wondering if I could manipulate answers with my mind and thereby control or direct the cast. There wasn't anything I didn't try. No question or throw was too absurd or too complex or too impossible. I even tallied the accuracy or inaccuracy of each result on a written scorecard.

During this playtime, I noticed a few peculiarities about using runes. Patterns of the cast would change according to how people *felt* about their question. *Unexpressed* motives behind the asking of questions would alter or change the outcome. Answers given would invariably address what was *most important* for that person to know *rather* than what the individual expressed a desire to know. Runes would work for me the same way they worked for everyone else *if* I was honest enough to be objective.

I came to realize I could not control or direct runes in any manner, even in my own behalf. They always took charge of themselves, obeying faithfully whatever laws governed their movement and whatever source guided the information given. They were not toys and I did not "own" them, nor they me. They had a life of their own and I accepted them as friends. In our friendship, we became a team of equals working together for the highest good of all concerned.

With the passing of years this arrangement of teamwork evolved, and the pouch was transformed into a "Medicine Bag," in the sense that it became filled with all manner of symbolic reminders of sacredness and unity. Native American teachings of "The Medicine Path," a lifestyle dedicated to healing and wholeness, came naturally to me, so I adopted them fully, integrating rune use into that worldview.

While later researching runic legends and stories, I found of special interest the tales of Odin (in Germanic lore) and how he "died unto himself" before runes appeared to him. Facing one's own death, whether symbolically or literally, was once considered a prerequisite for understanding the deeper meaning of runes. Tests and initiations were arranged which either simulated death or at least provided a situation whereby the ego personality could transform. As history progressed and secular needs increased, rune use altered drastically. What was once an earned privilege for the purpose of gaining spiritual knowledge became a routine skill for the purpose of marking public inscriptions. Secular designs and usages can be traced reasonably well, but only fragments remain of the older, more sacred glyphs and the method by which they were used.

The fact that the concepts of death and transformation were so entwined with ancient rune use affected me deeply, and I could not help but wonder about the timeliness of their entry into my life. It seemed no accident that runes came to me when they did, after my own encounters with death.

The coming of runes into my life also brought with it another gift—the return of memory and a value for things past, for beginnings and for history. During my youth in Idaho, I was raised in a Norwegian-like household that honored traditions unique to the Sognefjord region of Norway. Although runes were never mentioned within our family unit, the mindset of a people who once used them was forever instilled. Having lost any sense of personal history after my near-death experiences, I regained most of that memory, and necessary grounding and support, through the values runes led me to rediscover. They helped me, quite literally, to retrain how I used my brain.

After I experienced the miracles of heaven, runes returned me to the beauty of earth. This little book I now share with you is my way of giving thanks for that gift, and of passing along the joy of rune use.

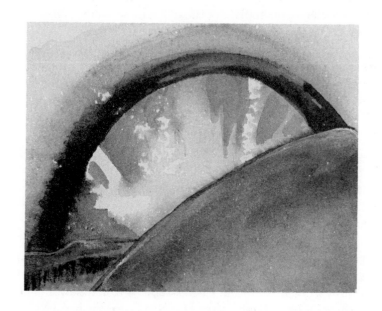

invitation

Within these pages I would speak to you of runes and the depths they hide. Though lately popular and described in many books, this ancient attempt at language provides more mystery than fact, for in ancient days it was unspoken, and consisted of many types and styles more akin to scratches and carvings than to words which flow through sentences and become paragraphs. These strange hieroglyphs, supposedly authored by fearsome raiders from northern woodlands, are older still than myths can tell, and the manner of their birthing remains forever shrouded and lost.

If you would learn of runes and their secret magic, first journey back through cracks in time to glance at what can be known of the powerful forces which may have shaped them. If you would learn of runes, be forewarned—for they are not what they seem.

Turn then this page, and dare to discover what runes reveal. . .

1
in seaRch
of ORiGins

Imagine what it would have been like to look above at Grandfather Sky's starry robe and seek to pluck a star, then to bring that star to earth by the carving of its image upon a silent stone. Such an event would have been no less than magic, for suddenly the stone and the star would be one, and all the power and all the glory of the star would now be forever captured. After the star, the sacred spiral would have been next, for it was everywhere present, yet untamable and unclaimable. Once again the magic would have come when this spiraling image of life's incessant urge to spin and grow was carved upon the stone for all to see. Incredible must have been the joy of this time, for through these carvings it was at last possible to hold a spirit through the making of its image.

Many professionals in modern times suspect that "star" was the first picture ever drawn and the first word ever written, followed by "spiral." Designs for both of these adorn more relics and more historical sites than any other symbol.

Regardless of how evolution arranged itself, once image-making was discovered and perfected, the skill seemed instantly to be everywhere. Endless variations of countless images followed. Designs were etched, sketched, scratched, carved, painted, woven, sewn, sculpted, and baked into and onto all manner of objects. Accurate records of Grandmother Moon's passage, and the rhythms of all the heavenly hosts, were knotted and notched as well.

Once these skills were developed, something else quite wondrous probably happened. Most likely by accident, image stones or image objects were somehow shuffled, scattered, thrown, or broken in such a manner as to create eye-catching patterns. Since all images were thought sacred and believed to be possessed of power, these patterns would have been deemed the result of no less than "divine intervention"—caused by spirits or guardians from beyond the visible world. They were "messages," if you will, of great importance. No doubt certain bystanders felt moved to know what these messages meant, hence the patterns were "read" and given meaning. Thus the practice known as divination must have been birthed.

Although numerous ways and means for contacting spirit forces and invisible realms exist, and probably always have, divination has consistently remained the global favorite. Its continuous popularity has insured almost as many methods for its use as people who use it.

Both the urge to record events and the need to retain ideas were natural outpourings from the skill of image making. Slashes and curves evolved into pictures, which then became symbols that formed hieroglyphs, the precursors to written languages and alphabets, cuneiform styles and letter scripts. But to better understand how alphabets emerged, it is wise to remember what is known and suspected of their origins, for each character assigned to each early language system was but a stylized version of some sacred image, nurtured by time and memory, enhanced by multiplicities of meaning, revered and held holy. These sacred images were themselves never considered simply "representative"—they *were* the things themselves.

Each individual character, besides occupying an alphabet placement and fulfilling an alphabet purpose, usually also designated a certain number, element, sound, spirit keeper, movement, star sign, and/or creative power. Early writings, then, were actually encyclopedic in the layers upon layers of information they conveyed. Since the average person was seldom privy to the entirety of meanings possible, the ability to read was most often practiced only by "wise ones." Today, we would identify these readers as shamans, priests, historians, or perhaps keepers of lore and wisdom.

This is why attempts to turn ancient renderings into modern text are so woefully stilted, incomplete, or inaccurate. In reality, older forms of script had more in common with secret codes than with codifying language.

Although recognizable types of scripted alphabets date back to about 6,000 B.C., scientific evidence suggests that spoken languages were common at least 50,000 years ago. Many scholars of language origins believe that a single ancestral tongue did indeed exist.

John Philip Cohane, an Irish etymologist (one who studies historical linguistics) and author of the challenging book, *The Key*, stated: "On the basis of the evidence, it would seem that a high percentage of the people of the earth today are far more closely related than is generally assumed and that they are bound together by at least one blood stream." (References are listed in "Resource Suggestions" at the end of the book.) Alessandro Talamonti, an Italian archaeologist now living in Venezuela, further elaborates that "a mother civilization was once basically uniform the world over. All people shared the same language, the same religion, and practically the same customs." Renowned historian and linguist Cyrus Herzl Gordon, in his classic work *Before Columbus*, makes it clear that not only were early alphabet symbols interchangeable for sounds, numbers, and signs of the heavens, but that they were a code language of unmistakable coherence.

Most scholars of pre-history suspect that around 12,000 years ago, language began to divide and alter as major land masses and migrations separated large groupings of people. Further divisions created what could be called a "language tree," with each branch remaining kith and kin to its original roots. For example, Sumerian is strikingly similar to Old Chinese.

As people traveled and traded more widely and culture was swept along with war, easier and more popular systems of speaking and writing were adopted. Northern versions in chilly climes were usually harsh and guttural, emphasizing consonants, while southern versions in warmer regions often displayed softer, more melodious sounds that clustered vowels.

Rune letters, it is said, emerged as sharp and angular from the Aryan branch of the language tree, one of several northern systems of writing. Believed to be a degenerate copy of either Greek, Etruscan, or Roman scripts by some scholars, runic forms have been historically recorded in three main styles: English, Scandinavian, and Germanic, with the latter dating back to around 500 B.C.

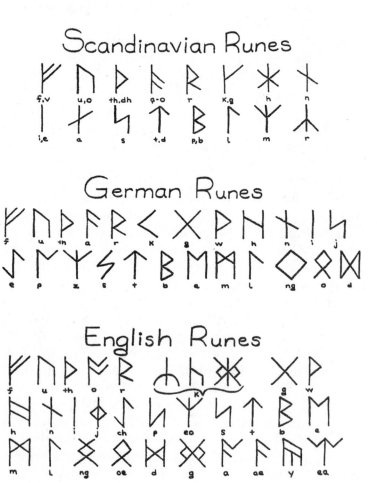

Among problems encountered when trying to date runes is the fact that runic script reads from right to left, like languages far more ancient than those of the Mediterranean cultures it supposedly copied. Glyphs almost identical to runes date all the way back to the first images ever created by the first peoples. These early rune-types are synonymous with ritual, divination, and sacred magic.

People from what is now southern Russia possessed an ambitious style of runes that were usually graven on pebbles or stones. Ferociously passionate, these people practiced the art of raising sacral power (later developed in India as kundalini). Their philosophy included an acceptence of life after death, resurrection, reincarnation, and the absolute value of truth and honesty. Evidence suggests that ritualized human sacrifice eventually became a common practice of their society, along with head-hunting, scalping, and ceremonial sex. As these early people spread across Europe and Asia, they took their beliefs and practices with them. (As a brief aside, scalping was unknown in North America until the natives here were taught the technique by European explorers.)

German, English, and Scandinavian people are descendants of these early fighters, as are Mediterraneans, Indians, Iranians, and the uniquely unusual Celts. This constitutes much of the Aryan stock. All their language beginnings are so similar that it is difficult to determine who really did what first. This can be seen in the amazing parallels between Icelandic and Sanskrit, for instance.

Before World War II, the despotic tyrant, Adolf Hitler, took advantage of what history seems to suggest and declared that the development of runes was further proof that Aryans were "the superior race." To add legitimacy to this maniacal declaration, he referred to the work of German scholar Herman Wirth, who had traced runic glyphs back 20,000 years. Wirth's research did indeed establish a progression of rune design, shape, and usage which seriously challenged any notion that the old glyphs were degenerate copies of anything. Although nothing positive can be said for Hitler's rationale, the meticulous research of Herman Wirth is impressive even by today's standards.

Certainly the Aryan temperament proved effective at styliz-
ing and systemizing runic glyphs, but the truth is that rune
images are so ancient they cannot be accurately dated. What
Wirth failed to consider in his research was the fact that no single group of people can claim rune origination simply because
every culture on earth has used them at some point during their
history. And, people still "remember" them, as if runes are
somehow a part of our genetic coding as humans. To better
understand the glyphs, one needs to recognize that they are
truly primordial.

The name "rune" is fairly modern as one reckons time, and
is thought to have evolved from the German word *raunen*. This
word currently means "to cut or carve," but examination of
older German dictionaries, long since retired from general use,
reveals that the original meaning of raunen was "to whisper
secrets." These older texts list the noun for "secret" as "Rune"
(always capitalized at that time in history), and further state that
the word can also be written as "Run" or "Runa." It is interesting to ponder whether or not some common denominator
might have existed between this particular version of the Germanic word for "secret" (*Runa*) and the ancient native
Hawaiian word for "secret" (*Huna*). Even though such far-flung
cultures seem to share no physical ties, their roots are not that
dissimilar, and their understanding of secret as meaning "the
mystery of sacred truth" is nearly identical.

Eventually, the "carved not spoken" language came to be
called *Futhark*, a name derived by combining the first six glyphs
of its alphabet in order. But in Sanskrit, "the power to manifest
and create words" is often written as *Fohart*. Did the name
"Futhark" really emerge from the random combination of the
first letters in a hieroglyphic alphabet? Or did it express a statement, perhaps an explanation of the power of language? Or did
these early groups of people somehow tap into a shared memory? Although answers are nonexistent, the questions are still
worth asking.

The "written not spoken" language of runes finally evolved
into a system for affixing inscriptions, announcements, procla-
mations, and various statements of ownership, record keeping,

and family history. Stone and wood comprised the media of use, with colors often added for emphasis. Later in history, it became commonplace for rune writing to include fanciful works of art which incorporated animal symbols, snake-like creatures, and ringerikes (intricate interweavings of vines and animal tails).

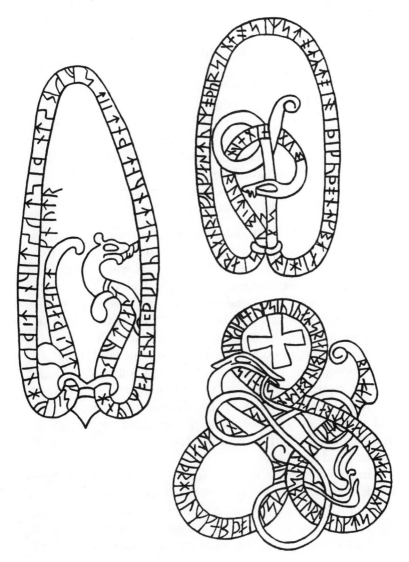

According to German folklore, the god Odin is said to have discovered the power of runes, while his Viking counterpart Woden (sometimes spelled Wotan) is given the same credit. Various versions of both stories are at least consistent in describing the circumstances of this "revelation." To illustrate the legend's basic scenario, here is a rendering from *The Poetic Edda*, an Icelandic collection of myth and story translated by H.A. Bellows in 1923:

> I know that I hung for nine whole nights
> Upon a windswept tree,
> Gashed by a spear and given to Odin,
> Myself given to myself,
> On the tree of which no man can tell
> From what roots it has sprung.
>
> No man served me with bread or drink;
> I peered down below,
> Took the runes up, shrieking took them,
> Then fell back again.

No matter what mythology you read from this period in history, from Finland to Iceland, from Greenland to France, from Norway to Germany, there is reference after reference given to runes: runes everlasting, runes life giving, runes as magic signs, runes to invoke the gods and spirit keepers. Never does anyone simply say, "I know my alphabet letters." Rather, they go on and on about how well versed they are in rune spells for any crisis, need, condition, or purpose. Even when runic letter script was well developed and in wide use, there was still no divorcing it from a mystical heritage of vast proportions. *Runes always remained first and foremost a magical language of sacred thoughts and secret deeds!* Their secular embellishment appears almost as if incidental, an effrontery tolerated to accommodate a widespread trend toward literacy.

In considering the multiple facets of runic evolution, there needs be some mention of the Celts. Celts and various tribes from the North, including Vikings, had much in common and often "borrowed" from each other. But along with similarities, there were stark differences. The following paragraphs regarding religious leadership help to illustrate philosophical and psychological contrasts between the Celts and the northern tribes.

Usually male but not always, the priest caste of the Celts were called Druids. They were a well-organized, well-disciplined, and zealous hierarchy entrusted with sacred powers of religious ritual for ensuring their people's fertility, good health, and continued prosperity. Another aspect of their duties was to establish and administer law-giving matters of state. These Druid priests supplied the only societal stability and guidance which existed, since the Celts as a nation never instituted any real attempt at unified self-government. Highly imaginative and volatile, the feisty Celts at one time occupied most of the European continent, and could easily have established a single governing body of incredible power and importance had they ever agreed amongst themselves. Their passionate individualism eventually caused their downfall, an end-result even their powerful Druids could not prevent. As a people, Celts were renowned for their courage and strength, unusual fighting abilities, and an inner fire which seemed ever on the verge of consuming them.

Because of constant wars, raiding parties, and the need to explore new trade routes, menfolk of the Northern Tribes were often absent for long periods of time, even years, necessitating the emergence of women practitioners as religious leaders and lawgivers. These practitioners, although not always women, followed older shamanistic traditions which emphasized the elements, plants and animals, and tribal loyalty. Ritual garments were elaborate and colorful; procedures intuitively free-flowing. Like their Druid counterparts, the Northerners devoted years to learning their religious craft and were required to pass test after test, including the experience of dying unto the self (transformation), before being deemed ready to assume sacred duties. From these women came a steady, cohesive framework that eventually stabilized and preserved most of their culture. Determined and stoic, resourceful yet daring, the Northerners as a people were famous for finding practical solutions to life's many problems.

Within both cultural lineages, the religious aspect of life was dominant and rituals were respected. Each worshipped a triune of powerful gods, plus hundreds of minor deities who varied in identity from location to location. These minor deities represented important aspects of their major gods along with the process of creation, both manifest and unmanifest. Since sacred law was not allowed to be written or recorded, priests and practitioners committed everything to memory, passing on the information through a series of apprenticeships and from generation to generation. Many beliefs were held in common between the two groups such as veneration of great trees, cultivation of special herbs, strict diets, disciplined personal regimens, the importance of wizardry, various forms of sacrifice, and a whole world of wee helpers (i.e., fairies, gnomes, sprites, dwarves, trolls, leprechauns, and so forth). As both cultures modernized, so did their legends, until today we have *The Tales of King Arthur* from the Celtic tradition and *The Tales of Valhalla and the Valkyries* from the northern and Viking traditions.

Druid priests are credited with developing a secret code which was originally used for private signaling between their members. This code evolved into the "written not spoken" language of the Celtic people called *ogam* or *ogham*. Paralleling the *secular* development of runes, ogam was refined into a twenty-stroke alphabet carved or painted along a straight-line base, with each word in a given message separated by space or occasionally by dots. This ancestor of telegraphy and the Morse Code would be cut or slashed along a stone's edge, using that edge as the base line, or worked into the design of various drawings, again utilizing straight lines as a foundation for each stroke.

Because of its stark simplicity, ogam became not only a written code but a way to use fingers and hands in signing messages from person to person. This finger alphabet was used in the same manner that we use signing for the deaf today. Barry Fell's book *America B.C.* describes in detail the varied developments of ogam and how often it has been found to adorn American artifacts.

The ogam stroking method which created alphabet letters from a single base line is as follows:

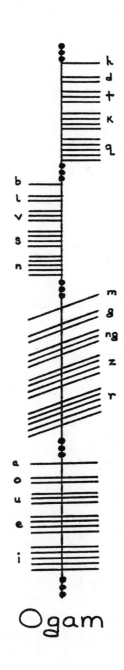

Ogam

Many a standing stone which bears runic inscriptions also bears ogam words. There is ample evidence to indicate that Celts used runes and Northerners on occasion used ogam. As rune glyphs seem to trace back to the first days of image making, ogam slashes likely trace back to that same time period as a method for keeping simple calendars. It is not so unusual, really, for Druids to have converted ancient slash and notch systems into a secret code. When finally popularized and widespread, ogam became the preferred method for writing messages simply because it was easier and faster to use. Runes, however, remained the favorite for ceremony and ritual.

When Christianity arrived, it dealt a death blow to anything which appeared counter to its teachings, and thus, much of what was once considered spiritual and holy was labeled "pagan" and therefore *sinful*. (The word *pagan*, by the way, simply means "country dweller" in Latin.) The Catholic Church invented the term "witchcraft" and so decreed any form of nature worship or shamanism as sorcery and the devil's work, forbidding its continuance. By the 1700s, ogam had faded completely and runes were barely kept alive by a handful of "wise ones." Eventually, rune use faded as well, and the glyphs retired to realms of folklore and myth.

If truth be known, it was probably more the pressures of economics, politics, and burgeoning populations, rather than religious tyranny, which phased out the old ways. Movements to modernize quickly labeled anything less than progressive as an "embarrassment." Metaphorically speaking, it was okay for humankind to be innocent of intellect and simple of ways while it was still fresh and new upon the earth but, once humanity began to mature and broaden its horizons, it was time to put away all the old "toys" and civilize. The current interest in shamanism and personal revelation is, in my opinion, an attempt by the disillusioned to regain lost innocence and somehow make simple a complicated world. The renaissance we now enjoy in rune use fits nicely into that need.

The legacy inherited from runes is more diversified than thus far mentioned. Apart from language, runes also existed as an art form called "runestone" which was once very popular in the decoration of exquisite bowls, cups, and platters. Historically, the word "rune" is also synonymous with the word "cantos," which refers to the main divisions in a long song or poem. Speaking of runes has always evoked a kind of poetic cadence which brings to mind specific scenes from nature and a reverence for the pulse of life. Although they were not spoken in regular speech, *runes were spoken in symbolic speech.* Not only were they spoken, they were sung! Rune singers were the ones who actually preserved much of humanity's early history.

A rune is an active image, a vivid portrait of some aspect of the natural world. Each glyph embodies feelings and rhythms deeply embedded within the human experience. Runes actually evolved as a way to capture spirit and preserve its sacredness.

To speak of runes is to speak in poetry; to sing of runes is to join in chorus with the music of life.

Perhaps this understanding of their power is why J.R.R. Tolkien created a type of runes as the ancestral writing of Middle Earth in his classic stories, *The Hobbit, The Lord of the Rings,* and *The Silmarillion.* Tolkien was a professional philologist (language expert), and he knew well the magic of symbol-signing. Nobel-prize-winning author Rudyard Kipling delighted generations of children by creating runic writing in his stories, most notably the *Just So Stories,* including tales of how the first letter and the first alphabet came to be. Although both men fashioned their own runic designs, their renditions are based on historical findings.

An old prophecy once foretold that the day would come when, through the hands of children and those with a child-like mind, the magic of runes would be rediscovered and returned to the world. Interestingly enough, before the turn of the twentieth century and again during the 1960s, runes did indeed resurface—as children's toys!

Children's toys, games, and stories have a strange way of disguising universal truths and spiritual wisdoms. Another familiar example of this fact is the simple game of hopscotch, which is actually a symbolic representation of the Jewish Kabbala (a study of spiritual mystery). Hopscotch is still played the same way its predecessor was studied.

Wise ones have always claimed: "To preserve sacred knowledge, fashion it for children and it will live forever."

And thus and ever has it been so.

2
RUNES
OF NJORD

To know of runes, to truly come to know the heart of their pulsebeat, it is wise to first become as a child again, a child willing and ready to trust, to play, to venture inward...for runes reveal themselves only through the magic of memory and the emotions of imagination. And, with this process of going inward, don't limit yourself to personal memories, for remembering goes back within each of us to the beginnings of time itself. If you go back far enough, this universal pool of memory will enable you to discover runic knowledge for yourself, as all that is already known can be accessed by anyone willing to do so.

Select a type or style of runes—any will do—and begin. Do not concern yourself with authenticity or procedure. Just play with them. What follows is an introduction to the type of glyphs I favor, along with what they have taught me during the many years we have shared together.

The set I have come to enjoy was designed to honor the old Scandinavian god, Njord (sometimes spelled Nord). He was said to be the god of wealth and seafaring. His children were the famous mythological twins, Frey, the god of peace, plenty, and fertility, and Freyja, the love goddess. Njord was never as revered in Viking lore as was his son Frey or the gods Thor and Wotan, but he was deeply respected, nonetheless, and honored for the prosperous, steady influence he was said to generate. Glyphs in his honor are easy to recognize, for they will somehow emphasize wealth, learning, and gain.

There are sixteen stones in the set: fourteen have glyphs carved on them, and two are blank question stones. The following chart illustrates the set, noting the basic keyword meanings for each glyph, plus the pebble shape which complements each rune. These pebble shapes are *not* historical, and are shown here only as suggestions.

The Runes of Njord
Basic Keywords and Suggested Pebble Shapes

Home, house, building. Wherever you spend most of your time.

Money, finances, salary, investments, your job. Prosperity.

Gifts, rewards, promotions. Pleasant surprises which come to you.

Beneficial gain, improvement, tangible growth, possessions. Learning.

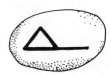

Comfort, ease, enjoyment, security, safety. No effort.

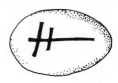

Negativity, poison, harm. Problems or difficulties, such as restrictions. A warning.

Change, a turn-around in affairs, an ending, death. Transformation.

Conflict, war, argument, difference of opinion, opposition, quarrel. Confrontation.

Confusion, a fog. Things are unclear, muddled, or irrational.

Family, marriage, children. A union or grouping of people. Community.

Love, support, union. Being together in harmony.

Fire, passion, creativity. Spiritual guidance, God. A sense of rightness.

Male. Man or men.

Female. Woman or women.

Unmarked Question Stones

Female Questioner.
This stone is shaped like a uterus
or an egg.

Male Questioner.
This stone is shaped like a penis
or a probe.

The pebbles in the set I use are small, river-worn stones from a stream in Mexico. They are soft-black in color, somewhat flat, and carved on one side (although both sides could easily have been carved). The grooves of each glyph design are filled with a coating of white paint. The two question stones are distinct from the others, being more rounded and plump, without markings, and of a different stone matrix. When all together, the sixteen pebbles fit nicely into the cup of one hand and are light of weight. In between use they are stored in a light-blue velvet pouch measuring eight inches long and four-and-a-half inches wide, with a drawstring top of white ribbon. The pouch is handsewn.

I recommend creating your own set of runes. It will mean more to you and be more personal if you do, because your set can then be a direct extension of your own life energy, a reflection of your own soul-force.

You can prepare your set from any materials you want, and design the pouch to suit your fancy. Do not limit yourself to my selections, for no rule of thumb exists except to follow your own preferences. It is entirely up to you how your runes will look and how they will be used. You may use them as a toy, a conversation piece, a game, or as a tool to help you understand sacredness. There are no dos and don'ts. Allow your feelings to be your guide.

Historically, stone or wood was the preferred material to carve on because each could handle the carver's blade and was abundantly available. Colors were often added for emphasis, but carefully, by pouring appropriate mixes of dye into each carved groove. Today, an engraver's tool or a woodburning pen can substitute for the carver's blade, and a narrow art brush can be used to guide the paint into place. Pouches were once tanned leather or furry hides tied with thongs, but today people often prefer different weights and colors of velvet or brocade, with cording or ribbon used for tying. I once saw a pouch made of fine needlepoint, complete with yarn tassels and tiny bells on the drawstring.

Regardless of how you prepare your set or what you do with it, runes take on "life" only when they are treated with respect. Your set will be little more than a bunch of lifeless, ridiculous rocks unless you set aside all preconceived notions and, like a child, trust yourself to flow with their magic. Rune glyphs are quite capable of teaching you anything you need to know about them. You do not have to second-guess their meanings or enforce any particular, ritualized regimen. Just relax and have no expectations. You need only a feeling of joy and a sense of fun and adventure to start the process.

There are some people, like myself, who prefer to invoke the spiritual nature of runes. This simply means choosing to hold them in reverence as an extension of the greater good or God. Although the set I work with was prepared by another, it is as if I had put it together myself, for it so perfectly personifies that which I hold dear.

Allow me to explain.

It would be unthinkable for me to have glyphs engraved on anything but natural objects. The idea of commercializing runes through mass production leaves me cold, although I recognize that such a measure enables them to be exposed to greater numbers of people. Uniformity of shape seems somehow a violation to me, as nature engenders each parcel of creation with a unique and different beauty. Plus, the idea of matching each glyph to its appropriate stone through a process of prayer and meditation seems to be the only reliable method, to my way of thinking, which can ensure that the vibration of each stone is in harmony with the glyph it wears.

My near-death experiences taught me that everything in nature is alive in the sense that it has consciousness, intelligence, memory, and responsiveness. Hence, I no longer think in terms of ownership but rather in terms of enjoyment to be gained through sharing, or growth that is possible from life's varied opportunities. Thus, the runes I have are not "mine" but rather they are "friends." I could no more "possess" them than I could possess any other life form, for only in freedom is intelligence honored.

Both the fabric of the pouch I have (velvet) and the origination point of the pebbles (Mexico) are of special significance for me. As a child, many of my dresses were velvet, and I would often stroke the plush pile, feeling as if its soothing ripples were a "hug" which the dress was giving me. I never outgrew this loving relationship with velvet. Also, in my youth, Mexican labor camps throughout southern Idaho were common, and the problem of "wetbacks" (illegal aliens) remained an unresolved dilemma. This disturbed me so much that I made a point of getting to know as many of these people as possible, later learning some of their customs and language. Although they lived in distressing poverty, these Mexican laborers proved to be unusually kind and generous, with deeply set spiritual values and strong family ties. Countless times since then, my life has been blest by Mexican people and the colorful heritage they preserve. I feel richer because of it.

This short explanation denotes my particular bias in the creation of a rune set but, in all fairness, the runes which I use have become more than what they might have been because *I* have become more of what I once was. We have grown together, the runes and I, as we have explored each other's abilities and potentials.

Even though I now prefer a spiritual approach to whatever I do, let me make something quite clear: *we make anything sacred through the power we give it and the way we hold it in our minds!*

Nothing is sacred by itself, and yet everything is sacred—depending entirely on how it is viewed and on who is doing the viewing. Just because I regard runes as sacred does not mean that they, in and of themselves, are anything other than symbolic glyphs. They are sacred to me because I make them so. You can make of them whatever you want. Should you desire them to be a game or a toy, they will function as that, and the magic of their meanings will apply in accordance with use. Invoking sacredness changes vitality, not validity.

Because runes are so ancient, they are deeply layered with multiple meanings and diverse usages. Each symbolic design is literally a slice of life captured through image and concept. Use of these symbols as an alphabet letter script was a "modern" innovation that had little to do with time-honored traditions. Actually, since there is no one way to regard them, there is no one authority on their lineage. That is why they are so magical: we can add or subtract from the concepts they convey, and still be right.

If you select the runes of Njord in the set you create, a closer examination of the symbolic designs will help you in understanding the concept each represents. The better acquainted you are with them, the more easily they can communicate with you. All rune types (and there are many) are simple and uncomplicated in the direct and honest way they describe life. For this reason, sexual connotations and life and death issues are approached openly.

In the following examination of the Njordic glyphs, notice how the designs flow into and out of each other, their shapes altering as the concepts change. Allow your imagination to guide your responses to them until deeper nudgings from memory begin to surface.

The Runes of Njord
Conceptual Meanings of Each Glyph

MAN: Open branches.

The upper half of a man's body was considered the predominant part, as shown by the emphasis on head and arms in this glyph. Man was the provider, the protector, who had great physical strength and knew how to use it. His was also creative power, hence the lower line extension which came to symbolize an erect penis (assertive projection). The whole design is similar in shape to the forked staff used as a symbol for Neptune—both the planet and the Roman god of the sea. Njord was a seafaring god who, like Neptune, understood the depths and the moods of water, and the ever-changing voice of the wind. Man's world was external to him.

WOMAN: Closed roots.

The lower section of a woman's body was given more importance, as shown by the floor-length skirt in this design. Woman was considered the emoter/producer/procreator, but notice the upper line extension, which reveals that woman was the equal of man in the use of mind. The floor-length skirt came to symbolize a closed vagina or a protected womb, but it also referred to great depths of feeling and emotion. Its shape, the triangle, emphasized a different kind of physical strength—that which endures (receptive stability). The whole design is similar to that used in other cultures to portray the reflective quality of a mirror (when inverted), and the trait of vanity. Woman's world was internal to her.

Man and Woman are opposite halves of the same whole. Both man and woman were considered equally important and were given equal status. Neither was regarded as superior to the other. In most Celtic and Viking traditions, for instance, both sexes had equal rights of ownership and of divorce. Man and Woman glyphs can be interpreted as either singular or plural, depending on how they appear when used in a cast, and on what feelings or sensations you receive when interpreting them.

LOVE: The unification of Man and Woman.

Man and Woman merge in the glyph for Love to create a single unit, for neither was considered complete without the other. Love in ancient times was most commonly held as the equal and bonded union of male and female energies, joining the qualities of assertive projection with receptive stability to forge a whole body complete within itself. Notice that in this design the male penis penetrates the female vagina and claims the womb, hence the idea of sexual love. But more than sex is represented here, for the bonding of opposite yet equal halves results in *true* wholeness. Love was not necessarily equated with passion by our ancestors; quite the contrary, it was thought to be more an ordering to one's life, a harmony, a bringing together, a union of little selves within the larger framework. This union was considered to be a support system which undergirded all future endeavors. Love was recognized as an expansion or enlargement of one entity into something greater than its original potential. The Love glyph resembles a Native American tipi. Tipis were designed to be flexible and movable, yet strong, stable, and lasting. By their very construction they allow energies within them, including occupants, to combine and merge rapidly, automatically fostering respect and harmony. The tipi shape emphasizes inner qualities while enhancing the development of those same qualities. Love operates in a similar manner, only it enhances and enlarges without boundary.

FAMILY: The combination of Man, Woman, and Love.

The union of man and woman brings forth children and creates family. This commitment or marriage secures a firm foundation for reproduction, nourishment, and safety. Notice that although children (represented by the two small circles, one on either side of the design) were protectively guarded by their parents, they were not considered "owned property." Each egg or cell was independent, complete within itself, an extension of the family unit, but not chained to or imprisoned by it. Ancient people fully understood that once a child was strong enough and able, he or she must leave the "nest" and seek elsewhere for whatever life might hold. These people also realized that no family unit was worthy or complete without love, and that love was the only true bond. This concept was expanded to include larger groupings of people, or the extended family—those with kindred feelings toward each other who may or may not have been blood or marriage related. From this basis, the concept of "family" was eventually expanded even further to include the idea of community, for without mutual respect and honor (love) no group of people could remain together for very long or live in close proximity.

HOME: The bottom half of Woman, with detached line.

Dwellings or buildings were often given female connotations, because stability was considered a feminine trait and hospitality an outgrowth of feminine receptivity. Thus, this design looks like a woman's skirt or the lower part of a woman's body. Notice that it is enclosed, fully protected and private, a sanctuary or womb-like place where one can feel comfortable and safe. The triangular shape denotes strength, endurance, and mutual assistance. Since Njord was a seafaring god, Home referred to a ship at sea as well as lodging on land. Later, it was realized that a person's home or residence could exist in more than one place at the same time. Because of this, the glyph depicts a boat on water, the detached line underneath implying that Home can be anywhere—even existent as a state of mind. The underlying message of flexible stability applies.

COMFORT: The bottom half of Woman extended out-ward; it includes Home and whatever exists beyond Home. It can be lying down or standing up.

This glyph illustrates a state of ease in which little or no effort is required. It extends the concept of Home and the safety of a secure and stable environment to include the comfort of joy and pleasure wherever it may be found. Hospitality offered implies the possibility of sex as a token of good will or as a courtesy. It is difficult in modern times to appreciate how important it once was to be safe and comfortable, to feel at ease. Just as the concept of Home evolved beyond the idea of a single place or location and came to signify a more flexible state of mind, so, too, did the idea of Comfort grow past any attachments to physical pleasure to include positive attitudes and a relaxed state of mind. "Easy does it" best exemplifies this design which, interestingly enough, when flat on its side, looks just like a modern-day house slipper or the shape of someone lying down.

CONFUSION: An aberration of Home. Not at home.

Shaped more like a child's disarrayed set of pickup sticks, Confusion looks exactly like what it depicts—nothing being clear, and everything being mixed up or muddled. The confusing condition of an unclear mind has been described as like suddenly finding oneself caught in a fog or a mist where details and landmarks are hidden or obscured from view. An individual can get lost without realizing what is happening. The process of living and relating can instigate feelings of disharmony and discomfort, as shown here by the irrational side constructions to the design and the abundance of jabbing points (illustrating that the concept of Home has been violated). Should confusion persist, anxiety and distress can threaten. The trick is to remember that fog is a temporary condition. A breath of fresh air or a good wind will drive it away. Confused thinking eventually evaporates and clarity returns.

CONFLICT: An aberration of Home: open conflict or war.

In this design, the symbol of Home takes on the shape of a horned battle helmet: precise, pointed, and erect. The glyph also appears to be a person with feet spread apart in a firm defiant stance—all senses alert and combative. The secure comfort of Home has been threatened. It is time for open conflict, but the manner of battle matters not—it can be disagreement, argument, quarrel, yelling match, or actual fight. When opinions sharply differ, resolution is needed. Opposition or an opposing viewpoint undergirds the idea of war, implying that sides have already been drawn and combatants are ready. Avoidance or delay is no longer effective nor recommended. War can be won or lost, but the exercise of "fighting" (facing a problem squarely) is necessary. A "battle" is at hand. Disagreements are encountered. Confrontation is the order of the day.

MONEY: Seed in a circle.

From earliest times, the concept of wealth was associated with birth and the urge to multiply manifested matter. This was, in effect, the idea of a fertilized egg. Therefore, this glyph illustrates a seeded circle, or a cell body which has been fertilized and is ready to grow and divide. The process of internal creativity was understood to be the "birthing channel" for all external results; therefore, those who produced and/or procreated the most were considered the wealthiest. It didn't take long for this concept to also encompass the possession of that which was taken or earned from others. Eventually, the symbol for the seeded circle (motivated inner potential) was "modernized" to represent the money coin, material gain, and the activity of dealing with finances, investments, and various sources of income. Employment and salaries were included. Both astrology and astronomy use this glyph to symbolize the sun. As the sun sends forth its life-giving rays in all directions, so the seeded circle brings forth and multiplies without limit. This is the idea of prosperity, of abundance.

FIRE: Abstract angle.

Much as flames create spontaneous, all-consuming heat, so passion was considered to be an overwhelming surge of burning desire. Similarly, as flames can run wild, scorching and incinerating all they touch, so unchecked passion was known to beget lustful obsessions which could turn destructive. Yet even ancient peoples realized that passion could also fan the flames of creativity, thus constructively channeling the orgasmic-like qualities of heightened sensations and unleashed power in positive directions. Eventually, Fire came to be regarded as a sign of God, containing secrets from spirit within its bright-hot brilliance. Note that the shape of this glyph is angular, bold and pointed, and slightly abstract. Its off-angle design highlights an understanding of a time when the concepts of God and the spirit world were beyond the comprehension of mundane society and often at odds with it. Spiritual truths were relegated to altered states of consciousness—moments when heightened awareness and the ability to know beyond knowing produced ecstasy, the ultimate passion. As fire is short-lived, so spiritual inspiration was said to be brief and fleeting. Interpretations of the Fire glyph were finally popularized to convey the idea of divine guidance and/or spiritual protection; but, in some cases, the glyph can still refer to strong emotions, passion, or the urge to create. A "rightness" of purpose is indicated by its connection to divinity.

BENEFICIAL GAIN: Two Fire glyphs, with a portion of each one extended.

This design consists of two angular Fire glyphs inverted over each other in such a manner that extended "tails" are created. The shape of a fish swimming forward, or upward if the glyph is turned ninety degrees, is the result. This denotes an addition or gain in one's life. In ancient times, the fish-like symbol also signaled beneficial actions of any kind, and times in life when tangible preparation netted tangible results. Opportunities for learning were present, improvement and expansion recommended, and acquisitions favored. Since Fire refers to the concept of spirit forces and the reality of God, the Beneficial Gain glyph also signified a time of blessing, when forward or upward movement was appropriate and spiritual approval was assured. Today, we would say "the green light is on" and better times are at hand. Additional possessions are indicated, too, because successful ventures usually reap substantial opportunities to increase one's holdings. It is of interest to note that this same symbol was used by early Christians to identify each other and is still held to be sacred by the established Church. Interpretations given by Christianity for this "borrowed" design are little different from those which have survived antiquity. The sign of the fish is the sign of nourishment. Because the shape is formed from two Fire glyphs, that nourishment can benefit one spiritually as well. And such gain can be profound.

GIFTS: Two Fire glyphs, open, with their midpoints touching.

Like Beneficial Gain, this symbol involves two Fire glyphs, only this time their mid-points touch to form an hourglass shape or a large "X." Two spiritual truths are evident in this glyph: the law of cause and effect (whatever you give you receive) and the law of correspondence (as above so below). But grace and forgiveness are also implied in Gifts, because of Fire's spiritual connotations. Hence, "X" marks the treasure trove. Something good comes and it is deserved. Gifts denotes a time when fortune smiles and pleasant surprises seem to pop up unexpectedly. Rewards are collected; things such as promotions, recognitions, accolades, pats on the back, prizes, or special items are freely given. Past efforts undergird these rewards even though Gifts always seem to be something extra, unlooked for, or sudden. "X" was the ancient symbol for star, the spirit sign of hope and joy, of promises kept and wishes come true, of the awarding of heaven's favor. When an "X" appears as a natural line indentation on the palm of a person's hand, the tradition of palmistry says that it signifies good luck and special extras in life. Gifts are pleasures to enjoy—whether they are qualities, behaviors, or objects.

NEGATIVITY: Double-barred cross.

The dagger is self-evident in this glyph, with both blade and hilt equal parts of the design. This is a weapon of harm, made to be used either by an individual or against an individual. A warning is intended by this glyph: beware of the dagger's point for it signifies problems, difficulties, restrictions, or outright violence. Dagger blades in ancient times were often coated with poison, making them doubly dangerous and evil. Even just the sight of one was considered an omen that fortune had turned away and times were ill favored. Poison used on the blades could also be administered directly by adding it to food or drink. Thus, the potential danger was very insidious, for daggers and poisons were easily hidden and disguised. As civilization evolved and such wanton violence began to subside, the glyph came to symbolize any form of negativity or negative behavior. This included gossip, slander, lies, cheating, being taken advantage of or put down, accidents, and illness. Today, the glyph is still a warning of uncomfortable times ahead. The nature of the negativity can be interpreted in a cast by the direction in which the glyph is pointing, and by which other stones are being pointed to or are nearby. Because the hilt shares space with the blade, collusion is implied—not necessarily in the sense of a secret conspiracy, although such could be the case, but, rather, collusion in the sense that there is often a "connection" between any given difficulty and the person involved in it. This connection is usually indirect and subtle rather than specific, and can refer to unwelcome words carelessly spoken, or a faulty decision that put others at needless risk. It can also refer to activities engaged in without regard to consequences, especially when these activities were the original cause of the resulting negativity. For this reason, Negativity, like Gifts, also acknowledges the law of cause and effect.

CHANGE/DEATH: Double-hooked line.

For a long period of time, barbed lances and spears were
used in war. If the initial plunge didn't kill an opponent,
then the weapon's removal did, for the resultant ripped
flesh and gaping wound most assuredly meant mutilation
and/or a painful or lethal infection. These weapons were
feared even by the strong, and came to be called "death
hooks." In this rune, the symbol of death is a double hook:
there is a barb at each end of the design, and the two barbs
point in opposite directions. The meaning is clear—death
cannot be avoided once an individual's time has come.
Ready or not, death wins. As people became more civilized
and mature in their thinking, the concept of death was
altered to indicate a time of change when affairs shifted
and life turned around. The hooks came to illustrate the
need for confrontation, the need to face whatever transi-
tion might be needed and then to make it. The glyph
indicates the idea of personal growth through transformation or through a definite change in one's life that needs to
happen. Movement is at hand. It is time for a change.
Although the Change/Death glyph can indeed mark a
physical nemesis, most often it refers to a symbolic ending
in one's life—"death of the old and birth of the new."

UTERUS

PENIS

UNMARKED QUESTION STONES: The shapes correspond with sexual organs.

Although not rune glyphs, these two shapes are important when using runes for casting. Ancient knowledge was based, to a large extent, upon sexual connotations and understanding the purposes of and differences between male and female energies. Maleness and femaleness were considered to be qualities and activities that were not limited to living beings but were, in essence, major determinants of how the world functioned. It was known, for example, that positive energy (male) and negative energy (female) were present in all things, whether animate or inanimate. The explosive energy released during orgasm was seen as a model of the kind of power possible when positive and negative energies were correctly combined. Realizing this, early people were able to accomplish feats so seemingly impossible that, even by today's standards, their methodology remains a puzzle. The sexual experience, then, meant far more than merely pleasure and procreation. It was used as a symbol for the creative power inherent within everyone and everything. In rune use, sexual distinctions were clearly made at the start. For instance, the asking of a question was considered "male" (outward projection) while the process of answering was thought of as "female" (inward reception, inner processing). Even for the casting process itself, proper energy polarities were established before a single question could be asked. This was done by using the particular unmarked stone which, according its shape, recognized and honored the gender of the one seeking aid or guidance.

UTERUS SHAPE
Refers to a woman or female energy. It is used in casting when a woman or girl wants assistance.

PENIS SHAPE
Refers to a man or male energy. It is used in casting when a man or boy wants assistance.

Runic symbols are not magic in and of themselves. Symbols are representative, not directive. The magic comes from the way they stimulate feelings, emotions, and memories. To discover them is to awaken to something hidden deep within the psyche, something almost forgotten. This likens to rediscovering a part of yourself—and *that* is truly magic!

3
the art
of casting

Casting is divining. It is one way of practicing the art of divination, of invoking the invisible, of touching the unknown, of capturing the secret depths a moment can hold when suspended in time and space. In plain language, casting is a method of throwing or tossing runes so that they fall in a pattern which provides an illustration of a person's query.

Every group of people which has ever existed on earth has practiced some form of divination at some time during its history. Even today there is hardly a person alive who hasn't tried it at least once. Most board games, card games, gambling systems, and dice-throwing practices are acts of divination, as are *feng-shui* (geomancy), dowsing, tarot, Star Gate, I Ching, Ouija, runes, pendulums, and anything else which depends upon "elements of chance."

Some divinatory methods are dramatic, while others are quite ordinary. Some involve sophisticated detail, while others relate best to shamanism. When people want to know more than is already known, to see and hear more than their eyes and ears can tell them, they use divination. With it, they are able to reach out and stretch past their senses, to perceive even beyond what seems to be the limits of reason.

Yet, if truth be known, the art of divination is really no more than a simple, direct, and child-like way of asking for help or seeking assistance from a higher source. It fulfills a basic human need for "parental" guidance and connection with a greater intelligence.

Anything can be used for divining "knowledge" from invisible or subtle realms, whether these "realms" be within yourself or existent elsewhere. A stone which is fairly two-sided will do. Just dub one side "yes" and the other side "no" and toss it. The side which lands straight up is your answer, like when you flip a coin.

The word "divination" suggests contact with divinity, implying by its very name that only divine or god-like spirits will respond once invocation is made. *This is not necessarily true!* When you invoke chance, what you receive is chancy! There are no guarantees in the process and no way to know for certain what or "who" you may have contacted. Practicing any form of divination is like opening wide the inner door to your own sub-conscious mind. Once that door is open, anything can enter. This can include *any* disincarnate, lower astral being, or thoughtform which happens by, whether negative or positive in nature. The key to handling this situation is to protect yourself, and the key to protection lies in preparation and intent.

The ancients knew this, which is why they taught stringent and sometimes complicated techniques for self-protection and clarity of reception, often insisting upon apprenticeship through a series of tests or initiations to determine if a person was "ready." They wanted divine guidance, so they practiced divine reception.

Unfortunately, excessive ambition and/or a desire to have power over others can cloud the best of plans. That's why many a divination ritual in previous times wound up as an exaggerated excuse to impress or frighten, instead of as a system for enlight-enment. Today, the same is true. Especially with runes. Perhaps because there is now such a renaissance of interest in runes, all manner of rules, rituals, ceremonies, costuming, sounds, and song are being resurrected, each designed to re-create and re-establish the mystique and mystery from times past. This is fun, and it is amusing. What results is like entertainment, but this makes it far too easy to forget what all the fuss is truly about.

Preparation for casting is not entertainment, nor should it impress anyone. It is simply a practical way to alter your con-sciousness and get in the mood for true divination. It is a way to center yourself within yourself, to "dust away all of life's cobwebs" and savor that which is harmonious, uplifting, positive, and spiritual. Any form of divination will always reflect your inner state of mind, regardless of what that might be. So the more honest and positive your outlook, the more direct and accurate your feedback.

Preparation does not have to be complicated. Whatever it takes for you to quiet your mind and shift your focus within an atmosphere of peace and joy will begin the process. Take as long or as short a time as you need. I know people who use candles and incense to set the mood, or who just observe silence. Others repeat the "Om" chant or do the yogic breath exercise of "A - U - M," verbally intoning each syllable slowly during one continuous outbreath. Some sing. Some pray. Some just relax and smile.

Inner cleansing is part of the preparation, too. This involves dissolving or releasing negative thoughts and feelings, and replacing them with a focus of love and light. You accomplish this by simply deciding that you are going to do it, and then actually going ahead and changing what you think and feel.

To illustrate the process of preparation, I would like to share with you the little ceremony I have devised for myself. I sit upon the floor throughout the ceremony, as this seems more appropriate and feels more comfortable. Before me I spread a white towel, which is used both as a floor cover and as a way to highlight the runestones during casting.

The pouch I use is filled with more than runes. Stuffed atop the Runes of Njord, and separated by a sheet of white tissue, are many small objects which remind me of sacredness. Having to remove these objects guarantees that I cannot touch any of the runestones until I first alter my state of consciousness. In other words, there is no quick way I can reach the runes. This may seem cumbersome to you, but it has successfully prevented me from succumbing to the force of my own ego. Plus, the relaxed atmosphere created by this ceremony tends to relieve any tension other people in attendance might be feeling.

I begin the process of centering within myself (inner focusing) by taking three deep breaths and releasing each breath slowly. Next, I begin to empty the pouch, withdrawing from it, one at a time, all those objects which symbolize to me a sense of oneness with creation. Often I express out loud what each object means to me as I finger and caress its contours.

Items are removed in no special order. Here is what the pouch I use holds:

A small bell from Bern, Switzerland, which represents to me the unity and interconnectedness of all people and all lifeforms.

A brilliantly banded, spiral sea shell, illustrating the perfect order of God's creation and the importance of water for maintaining health.

A small wooden egg dubbed "The Egg of Transformation," which opens to reveal a tiny human form inside. This says to me that there is freedom of choice. We are never trapped, regardless of our circumstances. We are always free to make new choices and to begin again.

A robust, smoky quartz crystal that is nearly pitch-black in color. This represents power, energy, and the living strength of this earth we live upon.

A fairy basket carved out of a peach pit, conveying the importance of our tiny spirit helpers from the invisible kingdoms who help guide form into existence.

Two hand-carved wooden angels, each holding a brightly wrapped package. The words "gift" and "talent" used to confuse me. For example, one person would proclaim that a lovely singing voice was a gift from God while another would call that same voice a talent. I spent years studying this paradox, examining it from different perspectives. What I learned is that a talent is something earned or learned regardless of lifetime, but a gift is something one has already become. A gift can never be taken away or diminished no matter how many times it is shared. With this in mind, I came to realize that I have many talents but only two gifts: the gift of joy and the gift of simplicity. Hence, two angels, each bearing a gift.

A crusty old barnacle, which indicates that everything in life is beautiful and purposeful unto itself, even those things which seem harmful and ugly.

A scarab ring from Egypt, which came to me via Turkey. This represents the importance of history, the ancient Mystery Schools, and all things past, for history teaches those wise enough to learn from it.

A Native American flintstone. This is a salute to the Native American viewpoint which I honor.

Two silver dollars, acknowledging life's abundance, and the fact that money and industry can be just as spiritual as any other aspect of life. Attitude determines value, not price.

A miniature marble from my childhood, symbolizing that the child within is ever present, and ever needful of being nurtured and of being expressed from time to time. The marble is a reminder to me of that fact.

A small yet exquisite cameo of a woman, which is an expression of my pleasure in being female this lifetime.

A hand-carved, rosy-pink tourmaline heart within a nest of cotton. This is symbolic of the heart chakra, the midpoint of energy located in the chest which enables love to flow freely and unselfishly. Because tourmaline is a source of lithium (nature's fabulous stabilizer and balancer), this heart also illustrates how true love actually harmonizes and regenerates all that it touches.

✷

As each object is removed, I gently place it on the white towel to my left. I then empty the runes into my cupped hands, and place the flattened pouch on the towel. Whichever question stone is not needed, I place atop the flattened pouch. This leaves in my hands fourteen runes plus one question stone (either male or female, depending on the gender of the person requesting assistance).

While still holding the runes in my hands, I affirm the protection of God and the reality of our identity as children of God in a silent prayer. I request the highest possible guidance from the light realms and beyond for the individual, affirming divine order in accordance with God's holy will. I ask to be of service, devoid of attachment, opinion, or ego. As God is the only reality, I request access to that greater truth.

While in this state of prayer, I sometimes "hear" how many questions would be useful for the questioner to ask. When I feel ready (relaxed, grounded, steady, at peace), I then reveal the suggested number out loud if it was given, and/or I ask for the person's first question.

I do not allow others to touch or handle runes, pouch, or symbolic objects. Runes move the easiest for me when my energy alone pervades them. They naturally retain a spiritual focus when handled in a sacred manner, and kept apart.

*

My own little ceremony may seem unnecessary to you, but it has proved its worth to me over and over again. Not only does it settle and center me within a cocoon of love and light, but it also has an amazing effect on anyone else present. A special grace seems to envelop everyone when pretense and convention are set aside and the wonder of child-like joy returns. This happens with runes. We return to our beginnings.

You yourself need no special commitment to use runes. You may enjoy them at whatever level of experience or involvement you wish and they will respond accordingly.

There are many different ways to employ runes. Using the oracle method, one rune picked from its pouch at random may give you guidance for the day or lend you information when needed. Or, on impulse, you may pick several runes. Or you may suddenly dump the entire pouch to see if one or more runes jump away from the rest as if to gain attention. Runes can "signal" by suddenly growing hotter to the touch or by sticking to your fingers as if coated with some invisible glue. Some runic systems actually operate better if used in this oracle-type fashion, similar to consulting the I Ching, the ancient oracle of China. The set I use, however, was designed solely for the more systematic method of casting (tossing as a set), so that is how I employ it.

Sometimes I demonstrate runes within a group situation, casting one question for each person present, in turn. Other times, I offer private sessions where in-depth concerns can be addressed. Occasionally, I use them for questions of my own, or for my family.

I always tell people, "The more specific your question is, the more specific the answer will be." However, this is not always true. I have been asked every type of question imaginable, from the vague and ridiculous to the precise and detailed. Some people labor for just the right words to ask in just the right way, while others simply mouth whatever pops into their heads. People will disguise questions, beat around the bush, ask "either/or," indulge in wishful thinking, or they will confront issues boldly and sincerely. In a group situation, most people are usually too embarrassed or shy to ask the kind of question they really want answered.

To be honest with you, the type of question asked doesn't always make that much difference. Runes have a way of answering the "real" question, whether or not it was ever verbalized. They seem to have a mind of their own which is more than capable of knowing what is really needed. If a question seems out of line or somehow inappropriate, I have seen the glyphs jumble up to the point that interpretation is impossible. Not only can runes answer unasked questions, they can refuse to answer any question at all! Runes "know" what they are doing, whether we do or not.

It is the questioner who must finally decide what will be asked and how each question will be worded. The questions are not up to me, or to anyone else who casts runes for another person. I request that no question be spoken until I verbally state that I am ready to receive it, and that I be asked only one question per cast. (An "either/or" question is two questions.) My eyes are closed for better concentration and heightened awareness. I always cast upon a floor, so that the casting space will be unobstructed. Table tops or laps are too confining.

When the moment comes that I truly feel ready, and the one question has been offered for the cast, I vigorously shake the runes in my cupped hands while repeating the question silently in my mind. I open my eyes, remove the question stone, and place it on the floor in front of me, about midway up the towel. Then I shake the stones again, affirming divine order, and gently toss them up in the air toward or over the question stone. Each stone lands where it will. Strength or force of throw is learned by trial and error. It doesn't take long to figure out how much force is too much or not enough. Casting has a special "feel" to it, and you will know that feel once you experience it.

Stones which land upside down I turn over so that all the glyphs are readily seen. Unlike with other forms of divination, the positions of upside-down and backwards have no significance with the Runes of Njord. I am satisfied in making that statement because I have performed many experiments to prove otherwise. All I accomplished was to verify the insignificance of any such dictum. In fact, it would be easier if the glyphs were engraved on both sides of the stones instead of only on one side.

The pattern formed by the stones in falling is more important than the condition of any single glyph. *It is the pattern of fall which tells the tale.*

When casting runes, no formats or layout rules are used, for such would defeat the cast. Casting is an experience in free form, without boundaries or limits. To do it successfully, you must learn to recognize patterns and to trust inner guidance.

Now, allow me to review the steps you would follow when making a cast using the method I employ:

1. Ask the person requesting aid to silently decide the substance and detail of each question.
2. When you are ready to proceed, verbally ask that person for one of his or her questions.
3. Vigorously shake the runestones in your cupped hands, repeating the question silently in your mind.

4. Remove the question stone and place it in front of you on whatever surface you are using.

5. Shake the stones a second time, affirming that what is most needed will come forth.

6. Gently toss runes up in the air, toward or over the question stone.

7. Turn over the stones which land upside down so that all glyphs can be readily seen.

8. Study the overall pattern formed by the glyphs around the question stone, using the question stone as your starting point and center of focus.

Rune casting is different from other forms of rune use because the technique of tossing runes creates patterns within patterns. Each picture or scene making up a given pattern contains many possible variations of meaning. Sometimes, several different interpretations of the same cast are equally valid.

Casting is of value if you want the larger view of any issue — if you want to see how all the many parts add up to the whole. It gives you an idea of timing and alternatives concerning the issue at hand. Casting has no value if you want to concentrate on single glyphs to the exclusion of others, or use runes as an oracle (in which you depend on one or several glyphs to give a single or separate message).

As mentioned above, the key to the interpretation of a cast lies in the pattern of the fall. This pattern gives you the slant to use and it clarifies the runic message. *The pattern is what casting is all about,* for it reveals the hidden dynamics at play *inside* the question.

One could make an analogy between rune casting and the taking of a photograph. The asking of a question lines up energies in a way similar to focusing a camera. Shaking the stones is like setting the shutter speed and f-stop while awaiting the moment to take the picture. Tossing the stones is equivalent to pressing the button and snapping the photo. The pattern formed by the glyphs as they fall around the question stone is the photograph. *That photograph captures the exact state of the person at that moment in time "inside" his or her question.*

The cast illustrates the *inner* environment of the question, showing how the stage has been set for each player and event to act out its given role. It shows possibilities and alternatives. It shows relationships. Each cast is valid only for the length of time required to make it. Since we all have free will, anything can change at any time. Nothing is ever fixed. Information revealed in the cast will *not* necessarily answer the question, but it will faithfully and accurately portray what the questioner is dealing with and what choices can be made.

Casting is an exercise in objective clarity and detachment.

There are people who use runes for fortune telling. But, since fortunes easily change when new choices are made, fortune telling is a waste of time. Too often such activity either misleads or misinforms, programming people's minds instead of liberating them. Free will—the right of each person to choose and choose again—should be respected. "Fortune telling," if truth be known, is a joke we play on ourselves when trying to avoid the responsibility of facing the consequences of our actions.

Learning how to interpret a cast means learning *how* to speak about what you see, as well as learning how to discern meanings. We are all responsible for how we use language, especially in our dealings with others. People are receptive and inclined to trust whatever you tell them when they are relaxed. Careful choice of words is important. For example, should it appear that runes warn of dire events ahead, do not blurt out that calamity is about to strike. Instead, ask a few questions, prod a little, find out anything pertinent, then emphasize approaches to whatever might seem to be the problem.

Again, remember that the future is never fixed. We may see "shadows" or indications of what might come to pass, but everything in life is subject to change.

Sometimes runes are easy to interpret and sometimes they are not. Patterns can be confusing, and we can jump to conclusions or make invalid assumptions. But, sometimes, what we see for the future is exactly what happens. Regardless of outcome, however, you have *no* right to frighten or pre-program anyone. Warn them if you must, but watch your words. Warnings can be helpful but, all too often, they become self-fulfilling prophecies. The more we think about something, especially in fear or anger, the more assuredly we draw it to us. Responsible speech and positive behavior are worth cultivating, if for no other reason than the fact that life returns to us whatever we give it.

After more than a decade of casting runes, I have found that I cannot change the patterns they form, but I can change the "eyes" through which I see them. I cannot control what *they* "say," but I can control what *I* say.

The easiest way to decipher runic messages is to begin with the question stone and observe how the glyphs arrange themselves around it. Those furthest away from it are further in the future. Any runes which scooted out of sight during the cast are not involved in the interpretation and should be retired to the pouch. Any which are bunched together need to remain so, although those which are glyph-side down need to be turned over while their original placements within the pile are maintained. Spaces between glyphs are important, so be careful not to alter them.

Your vision will naturally tend to move in predictable ways once you begin to study runic patterns and interrelationships. There are two primary modes of observation you will use. Either your eyes will seem to trace lines radiating from the question stone, or your vision will seem to rotate around this stone, circling again and again as if it is spiraling. These vision modes are not only natural, they are quite necessary. By using one or both modes, you will more easily connect ideas and thoughts with meaning. Undisciplined eyes will search willy-nilly for what there is to see, missing the patterns or patterns within patterns.

Perhaps these two modes of vision are related to the power of image-making and the days of our first beginnings, for history seems to indicate that the star and the spiral are the most universal and most primordial of any designs, as well as being the most deeply embedded within our collective subconscious. But, whatever the reason, when your vision radiates out from or encircles the question stone, you will pick up accurate information more quickly. Discipline your eyes and you will free your inner vision. Guidance comes from trust.

Here are some general tips to help you begin interpreting messages from a cast:

Always begin by looking at the glyph or glyphs closest to the question stone, and then radiate or circle out from there. Do not begin elsewhere or jump around indiscriminately.

Look for patterns within patterns. There will always be one overall design or theme, but individual glyphs may form peculiar mini-patterns of their own, offering extra information and, sometimes, hidden insights.

Notice which glyphs are next to each other. For instance, do all the negative glyphs and all the positive glyphs stay within reach of their own kind, or are they intermingled? Does one type of glyph fence in the question stone, while perhaps another kind encircles it further out?

Look at the distance between stones as a way to measure time. All indications of timing are approximate and based on estimates; however, an inch is usually equal to about a month. Glyphs which are atop or nudged against the question stone are *right now,* or at least of immediate importance. Always measure distance from the question stone outward.

Notice the glyph of Negativity. Where does it point? Toward the question stone? Away from the question stone? To nothing at all? Where? And what is it next to?

Observe the glyph of Change and transformation. Does it divide the other glyphs in any way, as if separating or sectioning off groups or phases?

Man and Woman glyphs do not refer to the questioner, but rather to other people in the questioner's life. Also, the Family glyph may not necessarily refer to marriage or to children. It may symbolize a group of people or supportive friends (the extended family).

Look for the Fire glyph. It represents the creative urge

and passion, but its refined meaning has to do with the spiritual life and the spiritual quest, an awareness of God. For this reason, I often consider it a signal of "rightness," showing whether or not a given activity or person is "right" or "on course" for the questioner.

Invariably, each cast may be read in several ways. Sometimes, the more involved you get, the more involved the questioner gets, and an in-depth dialogue results. Many times I have read from a single cast for over an hour. Interpreting rune casts is similar to interpreting dreams. There are at least three levels to every dream and sometimes four, corresponding to our physical, mental, emotional, and spiritual natures. Runes are no exception.

Some rune messages are blunt and short, especially if the individual has asked a yes-or-no question. With these, you find the answer either from a glyph atop the question stone, a glyph next to the question stone, or a certain type of glyph encircling the question stone. Sometimes negative glyphs can make the answer clear by themselves. Seldom is there need for much discussion with yes-or-no questions.

Rune casting stimulates the intuition. Since the intuition (associated with the right-brain hemisphere or subconscious mind) thrives on abstractions, imagery, and symbols, it is the ideal channel or thought mode to understand runic interplays. Intuitive guidance usually comes in quick, sudden flashes or strong feelings from the gut. Be open to these responses and give them credence.

When handling runes, remember this fact: they were originally symbolic images which later became hieroglyphs. They were not single words or single letters of an alphabet. The idea of a written language evolved later in history. Because of this, each picture symbol has a range of meanings rather than a clear-cut definition. It may take you awhile to become comfortable with this and familiar with possible variations. Runes are very cooperative, though, and they have a way of helping you along by instigating temperature changes or tingling sensations to convey information when you touch them. Various other mannerisms may also be employed to catch your attention. The more you handle runes, the more lively and expressive they become.

Experiment. Play. Explore. They love it, and so will you.

4
samples
to consider

Learning how to interpret a cast is like learning how to use your own subconscious mind. It is an exercise in trusting intuition, in probing the depths of your own being in order to access that pure, clear "voice" within you. This voice is the part of all of us which is objective, non-judgmental, and which loves without conditions or expectations.

The experience will challenge you and stretch your intuitive abilities as you seek to find that "right" feeling, that subtle nudge which unlocks meanings and messages. Casting is especially helpful in developing the virtue of patience because, during the process, you learn how to wait, watch, relax, listen, focus, and receive. The human ego blocks this "flow" if you hurry or allow too many interruptions, or if you are tired or ill or uncomfortable.

In casting, you don't so much seek for answers as you seek for that easy, quiet place of peace and harmony within yourself. It is an experience of "divine expectancy" rather than a search for definitive details. You trust and feel—rather than think or analyze. You *allow!*

Casting teaches you how to allow the Real Self, the inner you, to surface.

I feel it would be presumptuous here to detail page after page of casting instructions, for all you would receive would be my own opinion of events out of context from the environment which birthed them. In order for a cast to be effective, it needs the impetus of the moment in which it is happening and the combined energies of everyone involved. These dynamics heighten perception and enhance accuracy. Under such conditions, needed messages seem to burst forth, as when a petcock is removed to release steam from a pressure cooker. These dynamics are natural and unforced, and they are unique to each particular casting situation. It would be impossible to recreate this kind of scenario on paper. Plus, by overdwelling on my own ideas of interpretive dos and don'ts, I would in effect be limiting or stifling your own creative impulses—which are just as valid as mine.

I will, however, share some actual sessions I have had and make a few suggestions about interpretation. I do this with the idea of giving you samples to consider. Sometimes, when you see what someone else has done, you can more easily do it yourself. Study each sample, noticing the arrangement of the throw and any patterns that are present. Before you read how I have interpreted the cast, ask yourself how you would do it. Imagine what you would say to the person involved who asked the question. Look for several different ways to read each throw. *Seek for layers of meaning,* rather than rigid replies.

Ofttimes I involve questioners in the answering process, allowing them to participate with me in tossing ideas around. It never ceases to amaze me how quickly the questioner can fit puzzle pieces together if he or she is given a few hints. Remember, that individual knows his or her life better than you do. Also remember—runes are not "crystal balls." They are helpful facilitators of subconscious guidance, and they can inspire your questioner as well as you.

What follows are by no means complete evaluations of the sample casts, but brief outlines of how I work with runes and how I arrive at the information given. There are no set rules to learn besides the general instructions already given. Just practice, trust, and experiment.

And don't hurry!

Sample A

In my experiences with rune casting, some of the most popular questions asked are: What is the best pathway for me to take during the next six months? Or, What will the coming year be like for me on all levels of my being? The following case involves this type of question. A middle-aged woman who had just recovered from a serious illness was contemplating making several lifestyle changes and possibly seeking employment. Her question was, "What is the best course for me to take during the next six months?"

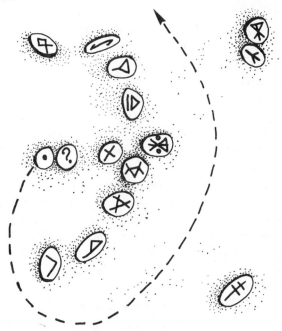

THE CAST

The question stone is female. The long curving arrow shows the spiral vision line I took. Since the Money stone is next to the question stone, finances are obviously the theme of this cast and the woman's greatest concern, although this was unstated. Notice, however, that if you radiate straight out from the Money glyph, you encounter Gifts and Family, with Conflict in between them. Next to Conflict is Confusion. These placements indicate that her financial concerns may be of her own making and not a literal fact. The situation in her home appears to be supportive. Also, notice that the Negativity glyph points to no other glyphs, yet aims in the direction of the past or the empty space below (possibly to the life phase previous to this one). At the top of the glyph line-up is Change, bounded by Beneficial Gain on one side and the Love of a Man on the other. She is headed toward making some substantial changes that will be beneficial and will meet with the approval of the man she loves. These key points told me all I needed to know.

INTERPRETATION

Reading from the bottom up, I pointed out that the worst was over and she could relax (Negativity pointing out and down). It was okay (Fire) to think in terms of future changes and employment, but not to hurry. She was still healing and needed more time. I suggested that she might think of some business she could operate out of her home (Home so close to Gifts and Family), or some product she could produce there. I counseled her that there might be many anxious moments and some arguments about what to do (Conflict next to Gifts and Family, plus Confusion), but not to worry, as everything was basically comfortable (Fire and Comfort aligned) and there was a certain rightness (Fire) to the way her life was moving. I spent some time assuring her that money was simply not the problem she thought it was (Gifts near the question stone). It seemed to me that as time went along there would be a woman or women (Woman) who would offer classes or services (near Change and Beneficial Gain) which she would be wise to take advantage of. At the end of six months (vision line about six inches long), she would be healthier, stronger, and better able to make the kind of changes she wanted. These changes would be blest by her husband's cooperation and support (Man, Love).

RESPONSE AND RESULTS

As it turned out, the worst was indeed over and the woman's worries over finances were strictly of her own making. What she needed most was rest and recuperation. Because of our dialogue, she began to think seriously about implementing an idea she had had for some time of operating a home for convalescent men (she had never mentioned such an idea during the interpretation). She busied herself immediately after our session with researching proper steps for licensure and legal medical affiliations, instead of wasting her precious energy in needless worry. Her husband was very supportive and, with his blessing, she enrolled in several appropriate classes, all taught by women. The last I heard, she had activated her goal, obtained all necessary licenses, and signed up for her first two boarders— injured veterans from the Vietnam *conflict*. (Notice how her boarders match exactly the placement of Conflict surrounded by Gifts, Family, Home, and Confusion. In this case Conflict was not negative, but representative of the men, like Gifts, who would live in her home.)

Sample B
Love and marriage are topics of eternal interest. This attractive young woman asked, "What must I do to get married?"

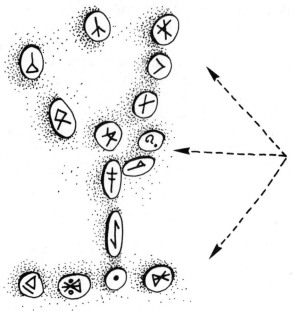

THE CAST

The question stone is female. Arrows indicate my lines of vision radiating from the question stone. This is one of the most unusual casts I have ever done, in that runes form the exact shape of a chalice or goblet, with the Man or men in the woman's life suspended over the chalice cup. In a direct line below Man is a line-up of Conflict, Negativity, Change, and Money. Comfort is at variance to the line-up, next to the question stone, indicating an alternative, a way to alter what appeared to me as a deeply engrained habit pattern.

INTERPRETATION

Before I began interpreting this cast, I asked the woman a question: "Do you have a habit of always asking a man's occupation and calculating his earning potential and future worth before you give love and happiness a try?" She became very embarrassed and her face flushed. Her answer was a sheepish, "Yes." Needless to say, this reading wound up being a good old-fashioned counseling session on how to form relationships and determine real priorities and values. The key to a change of attitude for this woman was the Comfort glyph, for it showed how love can never be contrived or forced but should always be free to flow in accordance with its own inner timetables. Comfort highlighted the fact that the only real security in life is what an individual feels deep within. External security is but a fleeting illusion compared to the steady stability that comes from self-acceptance and self-esteem. I paid no heed to the other glyphs, for the central theme I had seen was what needed the most attention. Details mattered not.

RESPONSE AND RESULTS

During our lengthy dialogue, the young woman admitted to a long string of failed romances and a short marriage which ended in divorce. Unrealistic views of money and employment had been at the heart of all her difficulties with men. She lamented about how, during her childhood, her father had drifted from job to job, never contributing much to the family's welfare, and had finally deserted the family completely. From this early childhood trauma involving her father, she had formed a deep-seated anger and distrust of men. I took the time to teach her several ways to forgive herself and her father, then suggested that if her resentment of men persisted, she would be wise to seek further guidance from a professional psychologist. She appeared visibly shaken, yet excited, when she left.

A year later, after several more failed affairs, she called to thank me for my suggestion that she seek therapy. Even though she hadn't been able to accept such advice at the time, she now realized that I had been right, and she had begun receiving counseling. As a postscript, she stayed with her therapy sessions for over a year, with incredible results: a happy marriage, a wonderful husband, and a bright and playful little boy.

Sample C

Employment possibilities and the work environment are important issues for most people. During one group demonstration, a middle-aged man, obviously uncomfortable with the idea of rune casting, gruffly demanded, "Should I quit my job?"

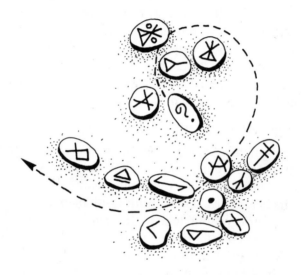

THE CAST

The question stone is male this time. An arrow traces how my eyes spiraled around the cast, beginning at the question stone and the glyph of Confusion. It was plain to me that this man was very confused and upset about conditions at his place of employment (Money in a line-up with Negativity). He had a good Family life and the Love of his wife (Woman), but there was definitely a Conflict at his job, specifically related to a certain Man. This Conflict could necessitate a job Change. Such a job Change would involve a major shift in his residence (Home), as well as in his place of employment. Nothing, however, was as clear-cut as his question implied.

INTERPRETATION

Since he was antagonistic towards me and flaunting aggressive body language, I decided to take a risk with my interpretation and really "lay it on heavy" with this man. In a non-stop, verbal barrage, I made it quite plain that I could not make up his mind for him—that the issue of whether or not to change jobs was entirely up to him. I said that in my opinion, however, his problems at work were because of a recent and perhaps continual conflict with a man he had not previously worked with, a man he did not respect and found irritating (Man surrounded by Conflict, Negativity, and Money. Gifts near Money suggested to me that this man with whom he had conflict must have received his job because of who he knew rather than because of any personal skill or ability). The questioner's job was basically a good one, which he probably enjoyed (Fire, Comfort, and Gifts next to Money). But I believed he was already considering a possible job change which would involve a physical move to another location. If he took that offer, the move would be beneficial and positive (Home and Beneficial Gain after Change), as his wife and family were very supportive and loving and would do nothing to impede his decision (Family, Woman, Love all close together). He would suffer no financial loss regardless of what he did. Both jobs were growth oriented (Money in line with Beneficial Gain). His question was not, "Should I quit my job?" I informed him, but rather, "Is it worth it to stay and put up with this new guy I can't stand?"

RESPONSE AND RESULTS

I would like to have a photograph of this man's face when I was finished. His body became instantly relaxed, and he crumpled in a heap. Seldom have I ever been so aggressively confrontive with a questioner, but this seemed to be the only kind of behavior he could respect. He was visibly shaken. After recovering, he described a blatant case of nepotism at his job, in which the owner of the firm had suddenly and without warning placed his own son as the new supervisor. Not only was the son incompetent, he was arrogant as well, and many employees were up in arms over the incident. For the questioner, the situation was even more acute because he now reported directly to the son. He had indeed received another job offer which would necessitate a move. Interestingly enough, this possible move had also appeared in his wife's cast, which I had done just prior to his (although she had asked an unrelated question). The man admitted to attending the rune casting demonstration that night solely because his wife had insisted he come, but he was now so impressed with the casting experience that he wanted to know more about divination and how this kind of thing could be done. He expressed an eagerness to pursue metaphysical studies with her, something she had been trying to get him to do for some time.

To my knowledge, the man is still employed at his original job, but he and his wife have gone on to take countless classes and workshops on human potential, altered states of consciousness, and self-development. Because of what he has learned through these classes, the boss's son is no longer a problem to him. This case is a perfect example of how the Change glyph can also signify transformation. What could have been a job change instead became a change in consciousness.

Sample D

A young man enrolled in college was curious about the coming summer months and the activities he might undertake, so he asked, "Should I move back home and look for a summer job?"

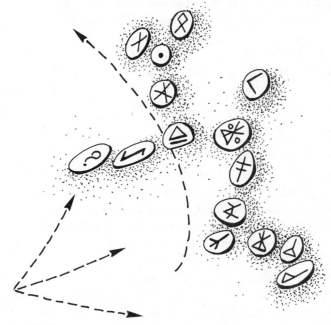

THE CAST

The question stone is male. Several vision lines are indicated. The position of the Change glyph followed by Home and Family indicates that this young man had already made up his mind concerning his summer plans. Notice his tendency to doubt and worry about employment as shown by the position of Confusion next to Money. Also notice a very probable conflict coming up with his father, as shown by the line-up of Fire, Family, Negativity, Conflict, and Man. In this conflict, his mother (Woman) would act as mediator between the two (Love and Comfort next to Woman).

INTERPRETATION

I joked with the young man about his question, saying that it looked to me as if his answer was a foregone conclusion. He admitted to contriving the question just to have something to ask. Since summer employment seemed assured regardless of his doubts (Money, Gifts, and Beneficial Gain together at the top of the cast), I advised him to believe in himself and approach the job market with confidence and enthusiasm. He would find what he was looking for if he believed he would. I then noted that there seemed to be a strange sense of conflict in his home, with his mother almost forced into the position of peacemaker between him and his father. I asked if perhaps the problem between the two men might be a difference in personality rather than a lack of love (since Love was next to Man).

RESPONSE AND RESULTS

Suddenly, as if some closed "doorway" had opened, the young man jumped from his seat and began a spirited dialogue with me, explaining how he had been adopted as a youngster by these two people, and how he had never felt truly loved by either of them. I challenged his assessment by pointing to both Fire and Love glyphs. It was clear to me that the family relationships were based on mutual affection, strong bonds of kinship (Man, Love, and Woman in a horizontal line), and spiritual unity (Fire as the lead glyph in a vertical line-up, next to Family). I reminded him that biological parentage does not necessarily make anyone a true father or mother with sons or daughters. Family titles are earned, not automatically conferred. He then confessed that earlier years with his adoptive parents hadn't been so bad, but now that he was in college, he and his father argued all the time. I asked him to describe how the two of them battled and what they battled over. During his animated reply, I picked up on several areas of tension which would benefit from an objective viewpoint of someone not involved. With this in mind, we spent the rest of our time together discussing the art of positive conflict resolution and methods for handling anger constructively. I was able to illustrate for him how he was just as much to blame as his father for their recurring quarrels, and how he could take the initiative in redirecting that energy into more practical channels. He seemed puzzled at first, then excited about the ideas I had presented. He vowed to make some changes—beginning with himself.

Sample E
Occasionally I experience a cast which is so dramatic that it is unforgettable. This one involved a woman who looked far older than her years, was critically overweight, and was barely alive from a whole series of health problems including a heart attack. The hospital had just released her. She was well known in the community for her unselfish generosity and her willingness to lend a helping hand to others. She was also an inspiration for having successfully surmounted many personal tragedies and setbacks in the past. Now, when faced with the toughest health problem of all, she asked a surprisingly blunt question: "Should I go ahead and die?"

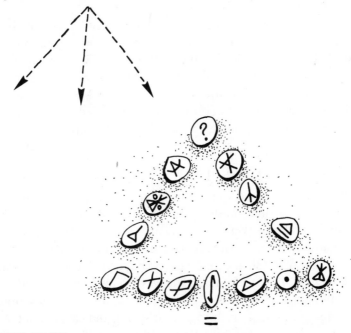

THE CAST
The question stone is female, and radiating vision lines are shown. Notice that the glyph for Negativity is not in this throw. It rolled far out of sight and was retired from the cast. The amazing part of this cast, however, is that Change (also known as the Death glyph) landed straight up on its end and remained in that unusual position throughout the session without falling. The

floor was carpeted, but not in a shag or any kind of bulky weave that would enable a stone, especially one that is so long and narrow, to stick straight up. The carpet was, in fact, quite smooth. Never before or since have I seen anything like it. It was almost as if that particular glyph was held erect by some unseen hand.

Pay special attention to the arrangement of the stones in a perfect triangle with the question stone as the uppermost point. Also notice that Love is on a second corner of the triangle and Fire (spirituality) is on the third corner. Because the overall pattern is so dramatic, the other individual glyphs seemed unimportant to me.

INTERPRETATION

Having had three near-death experiences myself, I felt qualified to respond to the woman's bluntness with more of the same. I simply said, "It really doesn't matter which way you decide, because either way is positive and either result will be beneficial. You gain if you stay, you gain if you leave. There is no difference in the result of either choice, so you decide between them. The question is not, "Should I die?" but rather, "What do I do about me?"

RESPONSE AND RESULTS

The woman breathed a sigh of relief, as if I had just released her from some terrible burden, and the two of us began a very powerful dialogue confronting all angles of the choice she felt she had. She knew of my previous encounters with death and, because of that, felt at ease to unload her own deepest thoughts and feelings. As it turned out, she was "weighed down" with an accumulation of repressed guilts, fears, and heartaches from decades of forcing herself to appear strong and capable of handling anything—a veritable Rock of Gibraltar. These repressed burdens, it seemed to me, accounted for her large body size. Since her life pattern was similar to mine, I had no difficulty responding to her. My son had once personally toured the famous Rock of Gibraltar, so I could share with her that the Rock was hollow and, like the Rock, our unrealistic desires to be superhuman were equally hollow. This statement caught her attention. Needless to say, our conversation lasted several hours, and I swear she looked younger and lighter of weight when we finished. Her choice, by the way, was not only to live, but to live life with a fullness and honesty she had never before experienced. This pleased me deeply.

Sample F

Some questions are so complicated and so outlandish that it seems as if it would take a miracle for fourteen little runes to have anything worthwhile to offer in response. One such question was given to me by a man in his early thirties. He described a piece of land near a well-traveled interstate highway. He and several friends wanted to develop this area as a tourist attraction. He pulled out a map and showed me the location while he continued to describe their idea. The exit ramp from the interstate led to a short access road which ducked under a bridge and then up a slight rise to a special mound of earth said to be sacred in the Native American tradition. Trees grew to the north of the mound but the mound itself was barren. Their idea was to turn the access road into a posted footpath. This would be supervised by guides who would explain to visitors the various markings in the area and the importance of the mound. His question was this: "What kind of signs should be posted on the footpath?"

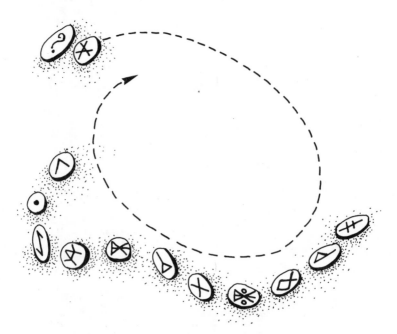

THE CAST

The question stone is male. For some reason, my eyes did not flow to the Fire glyph after Confusion. Intuitively, I was drawn to jump from Confusion to Negativity and to read the glyphs in a clockwise spiral fashion, one by one, ending with Fire. Glyphs for Man and Home are missing because they disappeared from the others during the cast and were retired to the pouch. Confusion reigns in this toss, with the remaining stones lining up in a serpentine fashion, yet my feeling was that each stone was a separate and distinct entity not contingent upon its neighbor.

INTERPRETATION

To my surprise, the glyphs seemed to respond to this difficult question by forming a "footpath." From this design, I was able to outline eleven places on the proposed walkway for tourists where either signs could be placed or stops on a lecture tour could be held. Reading from the bottom glyph upward, here is what I suggested to the questioner: (1) Negativity. This would be the staging area, where guides would meet tourists. Chances are most tourists would be tired, hot, perhaps grumpy, and not necessarily interested in any kind of sightseeing which entailed personal effort, especially outdoors without any protective covering. (2) Comfort. Here the guide would be faced with "winning over" the visitors, instilling in them a sense of curiosity and enthusiasm, and putting them at ease. (3) Beneficial Gain. At this point the guide could emphasize the historical significance of the area and the benefits of experiencing it in this unique fashion. (4) Family. Here the family life and traditions of Native Americans could be highlighted. (5) Gifts. Participants could be invited to pick up something unattached from nearby, such as a stone or broken twig, and bring it along to use later at a campfire ceremony. (6) Woman. An explanation could be given at this spot about the Native American belief that the earth is alive and is our "mother" in the sense that she provides nourishment and protection. (7) Love. Here, comments could be made about the Native Americans' sense of sacredness for all things (love and value) and how this was expressed in their lore. (8) War/Conflict. Today's more materialistic views of "me first" and "to hell with nature" could be compared at this point with Native American views of respect and honor. (9) Change/Death. Here, a campfire could be previously prepared for the performance of a short ceremony in which participants could, one at a time, offer their gifts to the Great Spirit. They would be giving in order that they might receive, releasing in order that they might be filled anew. (10) Money. The ceremony could end with comments on the Native American philosophy of sharing the wealth, and working together as a team to enrich the whole. (11) Fire/God. At the mound's base, there could be an invitation for visitors to sense the sacred power of the spot, and the specialness of both the place and the moment. A brief talk might be given on how worship and sacredness are an integral part of Native American life.

RESPONSE AND RESULTS

When I finished elaborating on the sign suggestions, the man pointed to an enlarged relief map and noted how the "footpath" created by the rune cast corresponded exactly with the physical shape of the access road. The points I suggested excited him and started a flow of ideas. Remembering the position of the Confusion glyph, I cautioned him about practicalities such as land use and zoning laws, regional park authorization, and regulations controlling historical sites and their development into tourist areas. I advised that a large cash outlay would be needed, especially for advertising and promotion. Although I felt he was being unrealistic in his aims, it was obvious that he was genuinely inspired and enthusiastic. Without discouraging him, I continued to emphasize caution.

A year later the project folded. The questioner had gone to court to stop a proposed sale of the land to a commercial manufacturing company, and was roundly made a fool of in newspaper headlines. In the end, new jobs and increased revenue won out over park preservation, especially after the media revealed that the man could not authenticate the site historically. As you can well determine from this cast, runes did not predict any future existence for the park. All the runes did was supply information related to the question asked. This information was based on the potential of what *could* happen, not necessarily what *would*.

Sample G

A middle-aged couple had moved to a new town because of promised employment, only to discover four months later that the employment situation was not as claimed. Faced with mounting bills and less income than expected, they asked, "Should we drain our savings account to pay off our debts?"

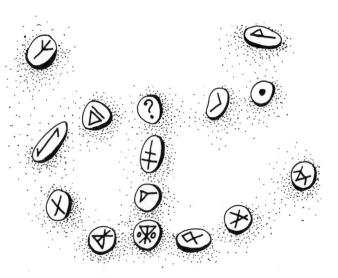

THE CAST

The wife spoke for the couple, so I used the female question stone. No vision line is indicated because, in my opinion, the answer was cut and dry and needed no interpretation. Can you see why? Notice where the dagger of Negativity points. In addition, the overall shape of the cast looks like an "A," representing "Account," fallen over and exhausted.

INTERPRETATION

I looked both people straight in the eyes and answered, "No!" This reply was so plain to me that I did not bother interpreting any of the glyphs.

I did a whole series of castings for this couple, and in each and every one of them the same basic patterning showed up, regardless of the question asked. This phenomenon is common-place, for if a certain message needs to be delivered, it will repeat itself over and over again. To illustrate this, here is one more cast done for these people. Pay more attention to the pattern than the actual question, then compare it to this first cast.

The question this time was, "What is our immediate future in this town?"

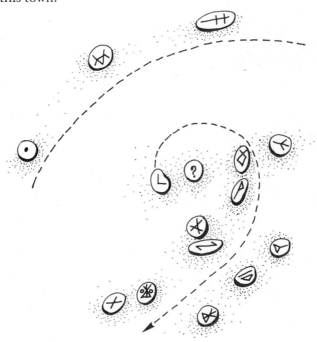

THE CAST

The wife again asked for the couple, so the question stone is female. Notice, however, that the cast is divided in half. The vision line for the pattern of immediate importance circles around to the right, beginning with the Fire glyph, but another important alignment toward the top of the cast conveys an over-all or future message. In comparing this casting with the previous one, notice that in both casts Fire is close to the question stone, and Home is near Change and aligned with Woman, Love, Family, and Gifts. Many times I have had glyphs divide themselves as they have here, forming separate messages or themes, and sometimes even addressing different topics or questions. This time, the message of the upper section is clearly stated.

INTERPRETATION

Since the couple was obviously worried about the wisdom of their recent relocation, I took the Fire glyph's consistent position near the question stone as a signal that their move was okay—that they were not to regret what they had done. Living conditions were comfortable enough and the husband was learning a great deal on his job (Beneficial Gain, Comfort, and Man together), even if his income was less. We talked about choices, and how it is that even decisions which appear ill-advised can sometimes either lead to other important moves or prepare one for other experiences that lie ahead. After making this point, I stated that in my opinion they would move again, probably in three to four months (Change three to four inches away from the question stone). But this second move would not be ordinary, in that conditions surrounding it would be confusing and unclear. Once moved, however, conditions would be better (the vision line ends with Gifts). In recognizing what looked to me like a warning concerning their future (the top line-up of Negativity pointed at Conflict and Money), I felt a need to be openly honest and simply say to them, "There is no money to be made where you are now without the constant presence of negativity and conflict."

RESPONSE AND RESULTS

The couple seemed resigned to their fate, because nothing seemed to be working for them no matter what they did. Even though their rental house was the nicest home they had ever lived in, and the area was a delight, both of them felt out-of-step, as if they didn't quite fit in where they were. Previously, they had invested five years in jobs which had been successful but had offered no future. Mired in the rut of complacency, it was only after their previous landlord had sold his entire apartment complex that they had been forced to move out. A wonderful job offer had then brought them to this new town, but the job had turned sour. Company management was too demanding and inconsistent. Many employees, not just the husband, were leaving the company. Both husband and wife were actively looking elsewhere for work, and were willing to move if something better could be found. This second move, by the way, showed up in seven castings, with the same runic glyphs at the same distance from the question stone in each casting!

Three years later, I was puzzled to learn that the couple had stayed in town. On inquiry, they explained why. Sure enough, four months after the session, with no jobs to be found, they had each been forced into drastic action: he obtained temporary employment several hundred miles away, and she went on a public speaking tour throughout the New England states. Leaving their rental home intact, they got by as best they could by renting rooms wherever available. Eight months later they returned, paid off their bills, found steady employment, and continued on with their lives as if nothing had ever been disrupted. This new employment, however, hinged on their abilities to calmly handle the strains and pressures of constant challenge—he as the new manager of a radio station embroiled in the chaos of previous mismanagement and internal conflicts, and she as a nationally published author on controversial subjects. In meeting what had once seemed a bleak future, they had made peace with the conflicts of chaos and were in demand for their problem-solving abilities. Both claimed that the rune castings I did for them were helpful, as the information given enabled them to take the initiative in altering the outcome of their lives by making different choices.

What had seemed to me like a dire warning about their inability to make any money without the constant presence of negativity and conflict (the top line-up of Negativity pointed at Conflict and Money in the final cast), turned out to be a "piece of advice" they used to good advantage. The "warning" clarified for them exactly where *they could make money*, so they looked for just that, and found it.

Sample H

An unmarried man three years into what appeared to be a thriving career in hair styling asked, "Will I be able to purchase a new automobile this spring?"

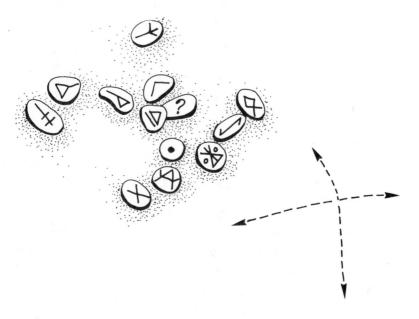

THE CAST

The question stone is male. Vision lines radiate. Love and Confusion were not part of this throw because they scooted across the floor away from the cast, and were retired. At first I involved myself more in studying individual glyphs than I did in looking for overall patterns and, by doing this, I almost missed the most important clue of all. As with dream interpretations, runic messages can sometimes be missed if you spend too much time concentrating on details. It seemed clear that in this cast the Home glyph could be read as the man's hoped-for car since it looked and felt like the car in question. Because of Fire and Comfort, it appeared as if there would be no real problem securing the car, although Conflict next to Money made it plain that price would be a factor. I also noticed an indication of a job change, probably beneficial, which would be a factor in buying the car by spring (Family, Change, and Beneficial Gain close to Money and the question stone). There are many layers of meaning in this cast, plus one, large, overall statement. I almost missed this one, and had to re-read it three times before I caught on. Can you see what I almost missed?

INTERPRETATION

First of all, I reassured him that he could indeed procure his car by spring if he truly set his mind to it. There was nothing really holding him back except probably cash-in-hand versus the price of the car (Negativity pointed away). Then I looked further and began to talk about his job and how it seemed to me that his money-base would change just before spring came, bringing with it a new place of employment and many doubts and conflicts over money (Beneficial Gain, Change, Family, Conflict, and Gifts, all in alignment with Money in the middle). Somehow, though, all would turn to his advantage. Worry was not needed (Fire next to the question stone). Connected to this situation was a woman who seemed troublesome but really wasn't. Also, a man might come to his aid—someone who was like a mentor.

RESPONSE AND RESULTS

The hair stylist had already picked out his dream car and was actively engaged in a loan search before he came to me. We began an animated discussion about choices, goal-setting, and various ways in which he could make his dream come true. He admitted to feeling restless at work, like it was time for a change. The more we talked, the more open he became, until he finally confessed to having accepted new employment two days before. Construction on the new salon was delayed but he wasn't worried since financial guarantees had been substantial. As I listened to him, I got nervous. Either this man was playing with me because he was distrustful, or he was gullible or naive. Nothing felt right. Something was missing—a link, a cohesive thread tying together the various glyphs—and he was no help at all. What was it? I took a deep breath, allowed my vision to blur in relaxation, and looked at the cast again. Details faded and the missing clue, the overall pattern revealed itself. Yes, the cast looks like a large "H," but what else does it look like? A square! Immediately I changed the dialogue. It was now my opinion that he was kidding himself about the car. He was literally *boxing* himself in with rigid presumptions and fixed ideas that had nothing to do with the reality of his life. While challenging him, I asked, "In light of your question, what does a square mean to you?" He answered that a square symbolized to him an economy model car or a used car (his dream had been a flashy racer with a price tag of five figures). "Is that all?" I continued. "Well," he replied, "how about stubbornness?" A smile crossed my face as I recognized the flush of red in his. As kindly as possible, I cautioned him to forget the car for now and concentrate on his new job. The casting indicated to me that all was not well, that there would be many problems and many delays with the construction, and that even once it opened the financial guarantees might not be honored. "Hold on to your money and be prepared," I said.

Six months later he telephoned. Construction delays had been incredible. There had been four months of them, forcing the new salon to open in an off-season. Guarantees were cancelled. What had at first seemed to be negative confrontations with both his former employer and his new one (women) turned out to be positive opportunities to clear the air and settle grievances. Because of my warning, he had scaled back expenditures and had managed to outlast the ordeal. The new job, however, proved to be worth waiting for, and it included the side benefit of a management training program provided by the salon owner, a man who became like a mentor to the questioner. The car idea was abandoned in favor of debt payoffs. "I'll get the car someday," he laughed, "when I'm truly ready."

Sample I

A successful middle-aged woman was concerned about her career. Hospital administration was her field, but in order to achieve her goals, a Ph.D. degree would be necessary. With this in mind, she asked her question in two parts. First she asked, "Should I enroll in the Ph.D. program offered at my present location?"

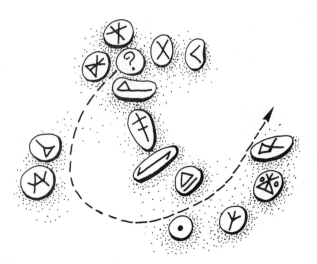

THE CAST

It felt better this time to allow my focus a counterclockwise spiral flow from the female question stone. With all the positive glyphs surrounding the question, notice that one of them is Confusion. Off to one side are Woman and Conflict, but pay special attention to the curving line-up of glyphs beginning with Negativity.

INTERPRETATION

It seemed appropriate for me to be business-like with this business question, so without fanfare or hesitation I began talking. Yes, she would like to stay and take the required courses locally

(Comfort, Gifts, Love and Fire next to the question stone). It would be very comfortable, convenient, and enjoyable, and she would like the people in the program very much. But, no, I would not recommend signing up. There was a significant chance she would receive a job offer elsewhere and move, making it difficult to complete the local college classes once she had started. Plus, I was uncomfortable with job offers in general for this woman (Negativity pointing to Change and Money), as she was so undecided about the whole issue. I mentioned the possibility of an argument or conflict with a woman before any move or decision about her future was made, but that this would not be connected to her business, and rather would be an isolated event (Woman and Conflict to one side). What continuously bothered me about this woman and her focus on obtaining a degree was that Confusion was the closest glyph to the question stone.

Her second question concerning this issue was, "Should I enroll in another Ph.D. program wherever I move?"

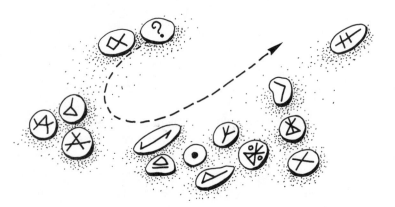

THE CAST

Again, it felt right to allow my focus a counterclockwise spiral flow from the female question stone. It seemed to me that this cast was divided into three parts: the answer to the question (as defined by Beneficial Gain next to the question stone), the isolated Conflict with a Woman (Conflict, Woman, and Confusion to one side), and the abundance of glyphs after the Change stone. Negativity seemed not to be of importance as it pointed up and away, yet it signaled to me that this question was not quite what it seemed to be, since it was the last of the glyphs.

INTERPRETATION

This cast confirmed the earlier one. It appeared to me that a move was a foregone conclusion for this woman. But, I again urged her to wait, to reassess the Ph.D. programs after she was certain where she would be living and what she would be doing. In my opinion, her future looked ripe with definite promise and a multitude of opportunities and choices, including satisfying male relationships, more job satisfaction, excellent learning opportunities, and career advancement. The conflict with the woman seemed unavoidable, but it was probably insignificant since no other glyphs were involved. It would most likely be an argument of some kind, or a difference of opinion.

RESPONSE AND RESULTS

The woman perked up and her eyes gleamed. She had withheld the fact that she had already received five excellent offers of employment elsewhere, all paying substantially more money than she was now making. She had delayed making any decisions about these offers because the local Ph.D. program was headed by a man she enjoyed being with and respected highly. Several of her friends were also enrolling in the same program, making it even more difficult for her to make up her mind. She admitted to finding the whole situation very confusing. The casting helped her to admit the obvious—that she was not happy where she was and that she was more than ready to make a move. She realized that an advanced degree program should not become a stumbling block in her pursuit of more challenging and exciting opportunities elsewhere. She would actually limit her future, not enhance it, by staying where she was—an important realization for her. The castings gave her "permission" to do what she wanted to do in the first place. This told me that her real question had nothing to do with a Ph.D. degree, which had been indicated by the strange position of the Negativity glyph—last in line, going nowhere. Her problem was low self-esteem. She didn't believe in herself. What began as a rune casting became a counseling session concentrating on her extensive skills, training, experience, and accomplishments— plus the magic of self-confidence. What she needed most she received—a big hug and a pat on the back. She left smiling from ear to ear.

Sample J

The following example is another love and romance question, only this time it was from a middle-aged woman who was divorced and had two grown daughters and a young son. She asked, "What is the future of my relationship with my new boyfriend?"

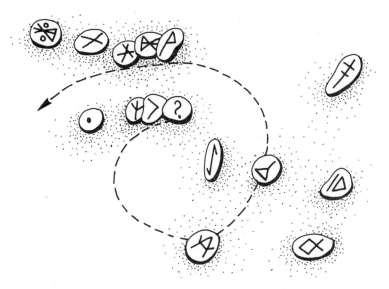

THE CAST

The question stone is female. It took awhile to decide how to view the cast, but finally, everything made sense when my vision line flowed in a spiral. Again, the glyphs arranged themselves in three sections, but intuitively I felt these sections to be past, present, and future. The present group is next to the question stone, the potential future group is above the question stone, and the past group is at bottom right. Notice that the first two groups have their glyphs lumped together, while the bottom right glyphs are far apart.

INTERPRETATION

It looked to me as if she had found Mr. Right (Fire and Man next to the question stone). Although it was not clear at this point, the relationship could easily mature into a comfortable love affair culminating in marriage (Comfort, Love, Confusion, Gifts, and Family in a row). However, there was a problem, and it might wind up being the deciding factor. Notice that Change is like a wall or curtain separating one section of the cast from the others. My feeling was that the bottom right glyphs referred to the boyfriend's past, not the woman's past. Therefore, the unresolved question was—could he release his past hangups about women? In my opinion, he had been hurt quite deeply in past relationships (Negativity pointing directly at Woman and Conflict) and he still carried pain, fear, and probably anger as a result. This could prevent him from any meaningful coupling, now or ever. I urged her to be cautious and not to hurry. The future was only a potential (Confusion) but the past was quite real and in need of healing.

RESPONSE AND RESULTS

The woman nodded slowly as she described his previous marriage, which had indeed been painful. Apparently, it was a particularly ugly divorce which had cost him dearly. Because of it, he shied away from even the mere mention of commitment, let alone marriage. Yet the two of them had fallen deeply in love almost immediately and could hardly stand to be parted. She loved him, but she was realistic enough to understand that love alone might not be enough. We talked for awhile about how some people prefer to retain painful memories as handy excuses to avoid taking future risks. The possibility of another failure can outweigh the equal possibility of a new success.

A month later the woman called me long-distance and related a slightly different tale. The man had actually been reticent about commitment because he had been living with another woman all the time he had been seeing her. He and the other lady argued constantly, so he decided to leave her. He had assumed that my client knew about the other woman, when in truth she had known of no such thing. Since the man had ended his relationship with the other woman of his own choosing, the questioner had no problem accepting the situation. This both surprised and delighted the man. He and the questioner are now dating regularly.

I mused about the turn of events and went back to my notes to study the drawing of the cast again. Had I been more alert I could easily have seen that it wasn't necessarily *past* pain and difficult memories holding him back, but rather a very present live-in lover. I felt foolish for not having recognized what was going on sooner, and I wondered why the terms "past" and "memories from the past" had felt so applicable at the time. The idea had fit, yet it didn't fit. While talking to the questioner I had completely missed another very important "layer" of meaning to the cast. But my advice had been sound, and for that I was grateful.

Sample K

Love can take on many forms, including a few that are unex-
pected. Illustrating this theme is what appears to be a typical
question from an unmarried business woman in her late twen-
ties. She asked, "When am I going to marry?"

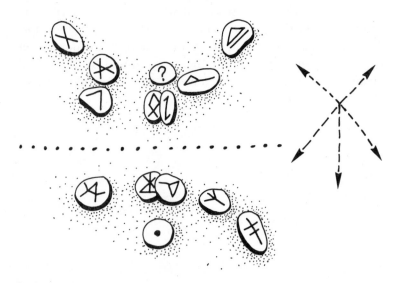

THE CAST

The question stone is, of course, female, and my eye focus radi-
ated rather than spiraled. There are two separate issues and two
different time frames in this cast—almost as if two questions
had been asked, not one. One section of the cast curves up and
is complete within itself; the other curves down and is equally
complete. Notice Comfort next to the question stone. Change
is atop Beneficial Gain and in perfect alignment with Love,
Woman, and Money in the section below. Family skipped off
and is not part of this casting, alerting me to the fact that the
question of marriage was not the *real* concern of this woman.

INTERPRETATION

The theme of this casting is complacency, plus the problems

inherent in being too comfortable (an easy arrangement of glyphs in the top section, with Comfort next to the question stone). I told the woman so. All was well and all was right (Fire and Gifts near the question stone) except for the fact that the woman was unhappy (Confusion between them). Life was good, she was on course (Fire), but there were doubts. A growing dissatisfaction reigned (Confusion), along with the possibility of mood swings and/or depression (Fire next to Confusion). In order to grow she would have to take a risk, a big one, which might compromise her safe, secure world (Change atop Beneficial Gain). Although the change she needed necessitated that she learn new skills and cut loose from her old lifestyle, the outcome would be successful. This I assured her. Fear, in her case, was a state of mind, not an actuality. The casting seemed to urge a change, perhaps a move to another location. If the lower section were considered a reference to the man she wanted to marry, then he was quite busy tending to his own problems, which seemed to consist of a love commitment that was dying amidst quarrels, feuds, and anger (Man, Woman, and Love fenced in by Conflict and Negativity). The core issue of his contention was, in all probability, financial, hinging on money and possessions. Although no resolution to the man's problems was in sight, it appeared that if the questioner moved to this man's vicinity, it might make a difference (Change and Beneficial Gain aligned with Love, Woman, and Money). This was a big "if," however, with no guarantees. But if the lower section was regarded as I felt it should be, then she might indeed move later, far away from where she currently resided, to accept a better-paying job in a lovely area. A woman's friendship and love would make a tremendous difference in making the move. There would be problems on the job, but nothing she couldn't handle (Negativity pointing down and away), and her new boss would probably be a man.

RESPONSE AND RESULTS

The woman's eyes grew wide as she expressed surprise at how accurately I had described her situation. She confessed to having signed up the day before for psychological counseling to help her deal with increasing depression and mood swings. The same day she had also registered for skill improvement classes. She was restless, yet she felt imprisoned by what seemed to be a life so good that she dared not change it. Her phrase was, "I'm stuck in a rut." The idea that the man she wanted to marry might also be stuck came as a balm of comfort, reassuring her there was no need to hurry, for he wasn't ready yet either. Whether or not any love affair was truly in her future, she was most excited about the prospect of a move and a new job in another area.

A year later, a friend of hers called and told me that the woman had indeed moved, after completing counseling sessions and becoming certified in new job skills. It was the friend who called who had made the move possible. Apparently these two women had known each other since childhood and were like sisters. And yes, there were problems on the questioner's new job involving petty quarrels among the staff, but they were nothing of real concern. Her new boss, a man, was exceptionally kind and easy to work for. The casting had helped. It had given her courage, plus the will to change. Whether or not this questioner ever finds the man she wants to share her life with, she became further bonded with a dear friend, and discovered in the process the right to claim her own future without fear.

Sample L

Life can sometimes bring harsh choices. This attractive but plumpish woman in her early thirties was born with a deformity which had necessitated multiple surgeries over many years. She was recovering from yet another round when she asked, "Will I have to face major surgery again on my left leg at any time in the future?"

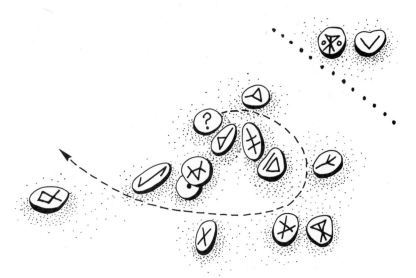

THE CAST

My eyes automatically spiraled clockwise from the female question stone and, in so doing, my first impression was that the casting had nothing to do with her question. The possibility of future surgery wasn't what was bothering her, but the situation in her home, involving her husband, her job, and their finances, was. Study the casting. What do you suppose led me to that conclusion? Notice Man, Love, and Confusion creating an uncomfortable Home situation, and that Family and Fire are far away in some distant future. The dagger point of Negativity directly impinges on her sense of comfort, security, and being appreciated. Normally, I do not consider the Woman glyph a reference to the questioner, but in this case I made an exception because no other woman was involved. I had determined this by asking questions.

INTERPRETATION

I wasted no time and minced no words here. These two people, the woman and her husband, must have been having difficulties for some time (Confusion next to Love, with Fire and Family so far away). This caused me to become suspicious of how long they had been together and why they had married in the first place. Common sense also told me that surgery costs had proba-bly "tipped the barrel" for them financially, thus compromising their financial security (Conflict atop Money). But with Gifts nearby, and Conflict-atop-Money so close to the question stone and to Comfort, Negativity, and Change, it was my feeling that their financial woes were existent long before her surgery. Stress, tension, and even shouting matches and quarrels were indicated. A divorce or separation seemed at hand, or at least some kind of change which could lead to Beneficial Gain. To my way of thinking, this situation was hurting her more than her husband (notice the dagger's point) and, if any split occurred, it would be at her insistence.

RESPONSE AND RESULTS

The woman's surprised face was soon awash in tears. "No truer words have ever been spoken," she sobbed. This latest surgery had indeed been the "last straw," bringing to light three years of money mismanagement, even though she and her husband both had good jobs. The disinterest and withdrawal of her hus-band had also become apparent. He insisted that he didn't know how to relate to her or understand what she expected of him (notice the alignment of Man and Confusion far away from Woman). When I asked more questions, I learned that the idea of marriage had been his, not hers, but that she had gone along with it so as not to lose him. The love between them was real enough, but neither could stand the other's personality traits or personal habits. They were destroying each other, yet neither wanted to alter their own long-standing behavior patterns. Her list of grievances was so excessive that I skirted the subject altogether, and made the following recommendations: "Since you are incapable right now of fending for yourself, and he is making no demands of you, call a truce. Give the situation another chance, and give yourself time to heal. Be pleasant and forgiving and bide your time. It sounds to me as if you're trying too hard and expecting too much. This is an old problem, not a new one, and it will not be solved overnight. The strain you've been under lately and the pain you've been suffering have intensified the differences you've had with your husband since you first met. In my opinion, neither of you knows how to communicate with the other effectively or how to listen non-judgmentally. If you want the freedom to make different choices in life, you must also grant that same right to him, unconditionally. When you feel better, pursue marriage counseling and/or classes in the true art of communication."

A year and a half later, I received a letter from the woman. Her husband had refused marriage counseling and classes, so she had gone ahead without him and done both. She had grown immensely from the experience while he had stagnated. This had resulted in divorce. She had then quit her job, rented a U-Haul, and moved bag and baggage to another state for a complete environment change. A photograph enclosed with the letter showed her to be slimmer, healthier-looking, and exuding a happy self-confidence. The divorce shook up the husband so much that he was apparently forced to reassess his behavior and go to a counselor. Both people gained from what had once been a mismatch.

*

These twelve cases should give you an idea of the process of rune casting, and the importance of honoring your feelings when a given question is asked. Please do not allow yourself to be limited by my interpretations but, rather, use them as a springboard for developing your own personal methods and style. What works for you is what counts, not what works for me. Do not feel you are "wrong" if your methods differ from mine. Experiment. Play. Demonstrate. Test yourself and the runes you use. You can only determine what works for you by hands-on experience. Runes do not work from your head—they extend from your heart.

I am partial to the art of casting because it is uninhibited and free of restraints while still offering a reliable "lens" through which infinite patterns of light and darkness, mind and spirit can be viewed. Rune casting depends on "flow" and a trust in one's own intuition. There are no formats, and no limitations other than those you invent for yourself.

Regardless of how you may use runes, they will faithfully lead you through the depths of the inner self to the primordial magic of sacredness. They will allow you to be a child again in a world which tolerates only adults.

Runes have a strange way of highlighting the subconscious *objectively* and the conscious *subjectively*, which is exactly backwards. This can be disconcerting until you get used to it. But, then, this is why rune casting is so much fun—it is completely unpredictable!

5

cautions

Divination is often perceived as being synonymous with superstition. Too many times its healthy truisms are cloaked in exaggerated or ghoulish practices, more a sign of ignorance and stupidity than an indication of ill-intent. However, since the word "divination" suggests contact with divinity, incorrectly implying by its very name that only divine or god-like spirits will respond once invocation has been made, the process is subject to every possible abuse and misuse.

All divinatory processes, regardless of their various methods, open the inner doorway to the realms of mind and spirit. These processes are based on the inner life and inner realities. But, for the uninformed and unprepared, who give nary a thought to possible consequences or outcomes, this "doorway" can lead to subtle entrapments that are more detrimental than helpful. When the known way dissolves, the innocent can get lost.

During the two years in which I traveled throughout several states, testing the first version of this book and the casting method it describes, I discovered people who, in not under-standing mind and spirit, turned the art of divination into a circus. All manner of issues surfaced for these people, from the ethics of fortune telling to the problem of possible possession by disincarnates (bodiless beings). I also found that there were a few things about rune casting which consistently confused peo-ple. These things were simple concerns, but in need of further elaboration, nonetheless. Because of these discoveries, I have included this chapter on cautions, which covers some sugges-tions and advice for those who seek to shine light on that which appears to be in shadow.

Here follow nine topics for your consideration:

1. SECRETS OF INTERPRETING A CAST

Three keys will unlock the secrets of interpreting any rune cast: eyesight discipline, pattern recognition, and receptivity to intuition.

A) I cannot emphasize enough that interpretation begins with the question stone. Train yourself to see it first. The scattering of runic glyphs in a cast has no value if the questioner's energy is not central to the cast. The question stone represents the questioner's energy; it honors that individual and whatever is *truly* the question at hand, be it spoken or not. The question stone is your link to the inner depths of the energy which splays out before you. From the central focus it offers, allow your eyes to radiate out or spiral around, catching in your sight the locations of the various glyphs. Be aware of any glyphs which skip away or refuse to cooperate, for they are asking to be excused from the cast.

B) Teach yourself to look for an overall pattern to the cast. A pattern may not always be present, but the majority of casts will have one. This overall pattern is quite literally the theme of the cast, influencing the direction and import of any message the runic glyphs might convey.

Go back through the chapter on samples and see if you can find any casts which have overall, central patterns. Actually, they all do, but some are more pronounced than others. Take, for instance, Sample B. In this cast, the chalice shape is plainly visible. It is a wedding chalice which the questioner wishes to drink from. But also notice that Man is suspended midway over the open cup of the chalice, directly lined up with Conflict, Negativity, Change, and Money. Comfort and the question stone to the right side reveal the only "right" solution to the question. This is certainly an example of a very powerful overall pattern with an equally powerful theme. Another example of such a striking design is Sample E. But overall patterns can sometimes be elusive and difficult to recognize, as Sample H proved to me until I finally saw the "square" which revealed the cast's true meaning. Yet, in this sample, I could have ascertained that the "H" within the square stood for "hard" or "Honda" or "hindrance," a clue which might have led me to the same conclusion.

In most of the sample cases illustrated in this book, I have left it up to you to decide whether or not there is an overall pattern to the cast, and whether smaller patterns exist within it. If I explain every little detail of each cast and what I think it means, you would be denied the opportunity to recognize what is there yourself. Ample hints are enough for me to offer. The rest is up to you.

With rune casting, meaning comes from patterns, not necessarily from individual glyphs. A pattern, remember, is a symbol or design that blends together many parts to form a whole. So always, always look for the patterns—any overall design plus major and/or minor groupings. Widen your view. Train yourself. Discipline your eyes to connect or link together what you see.

C) Any form of divination depends for success on your receptivity to the process of intuition. Intuition is that subtle wee voice at the inner core of our beings. It is our conscience, the part of us which knows that it knows—perhaps the very voice of our own soul, and of every other soul. Sometimes intuition speaks, for we seem to hear an actual "voice;" sometimes it nudges like a gentle "push" from behind; and sometimes it expresses through the gut or the feeling structure of our emotions and senses. Science tells us that intuition is a product of the right hemisphere of our brain. Psychics say it is the initial entry point to psychism and the development of psychic abilities. Whatever it is called or thought to be, intuition is an invaluable skill that is necessary, I believe, for a healthy, well-rounded life. We are not balanced or whole without it.

Men, by the way, are just as intuitive as women. The only difference is that women readily accept their intuitive abilities while men usually do everything they can to deny them. This has more to do with cultural stigmas than natural receptivity.

Free-form rune casting, which is what this book is about, nurtures and develops intuition. It teaches you how to use your right-brain hemisphere more effectively and it helps you learn to trust the abilities you develop. Free-form rune casting depends on the intuitive process to work. No opportunity exists in this process for a person to lean on the security of rules, regulations, or formats.

Through pure spontaneity and the immediacy of the moment, one is obliged to surrender to the power of love and truth, the wisdom of the inner self, the Greater Self, the God within. Because surrender of the ego (releasing the outer self or personality facade) is so necessary, protection of the inner self is paramount. That's why the ancients held rituals of cleansing and attunement before practicing divinatory arts. To insure proper reception, they practiced proper preparation. Short-cuts were not allowed.

2. HISTORICAL CONTEXT

Rune use recreates a sense of innocence and history. It provides an opportunity to rediscover what might have existed during the times of Druids, Celts, Vikings, and cultures older still. This historical context establishes a point of beginning—and it sets a precedent. But precedent can be tricky. Over-reliance on it can result in a mindset so dogmatic and rigid that spontaneity is lost. And spontaneity is what makes rune casting unique and allows divination its mystery. To limit the limitless denies the very spirituality you may be trying to access.

For this reason, I pass along the following advice about history, both personal and collective, and about runes:

> We don't go back to the past—we reach back to the past and bring what is helpful and useful into our modern society and into our modern lives. We have to live now; we can't live then. If we try to live then, we are in trouble.

These words of counsel were spoken by Dr. E. Otha Wingo about the spiritual practice of Huna during a 1984 interview conducted by Peter Young on radio station KKON, Kealakekua, Hawaii. Dr. Wingo is director of Huna Research, headquartered in Missouri, and a college professor of ancient languages. His caution is worth heeding. (Huna, by the way, is a practical system of spirituality developed centuries ago in the Hawaiian Islands. Although the word *Huna* means "secret," the system it espouses is applicable to modern lifestyles.)

No matter how hard a person strives for historical authenticity and no matter how thorough the research, any runes used today will still be viewed through the eyes of today, and tossed with the muscles of the present moment.

Wise is the person who learns from the past, but foolish is the one who clings to it.

3. OVERUSE AND MISUSE

You can use runes too often. Any divinatory skill can become a crutch leading to dependence and fantasy. When you ask the same question over and over again, you chain yourself to the "merry-go-round" of indecision. Even masking your concerns by rewording your requests for the same guidance will, if done repeatedly, net you no more than distortion or confusion.

We can sabotage ourselves by our own impatience. Our egos can take over, overwhelm the process from sheer force of will, and thus insure that our own self-centered prophecies will be the outcome. It is amazing to me how often people receive in "guidance" only what they want to receive. This is self-deception. And self-deception is the biggest entrapment of all!

You cannot hurry divinatory processes, for they are based on feeling and sensing, not thoughts. The purpose of their use is guidance, not ego strokes. The true power of divination comes from communion with the Greater Self. Complexities of ritual and perceptions of urgency can detract from this goal.

One woman I met had reworded her same question over and over again, casting up to three times per day, day after day, for more than a week, and then wondered why she felt so irritable and frustrated. Of course she felt that way. How many times must a person be given the same information before overload occurs and the nervous system rebels?

Runes cannot make decisions. They cannot decide the future. They and any other divinatory tool can only impart information. The rest is up to you. Choose, act, then face the consequences responsibly.

4. THE QUESTION STONE AND SEXUAL ENERGY

The energy of the question stone works best when it represents the *physical energy of the body* worn by the questioner. We "wear" our bodies in the sense that we are immortal souls inhabiting a human form while sojourning in the earthplane.

Throughout history and regardless of culture, this "physical energy of the body" has most consistently been portrayed as sexual in nature and creative in function. Yet, there is no evidence to support the theory that ancient people limited their understanding of this energy to gender differences and orgasm. Rather, evidence persuasively illustrates that sexual "models" were used symbolically to represent a deep and rich understanding of what energy is, what its basic components are, and how matter itself manifests. These people understood the secret of life in a dynamic fashion.

Since this ancient understanding of sexual energy is central to rune casting, and important to other forms of divination as well, I want to clarify what is generally meant by sexual energy in terms of "male" and "female" expressions of that energy.

Based on the Taoist principle of Yin for female energy and the principle of Yang for male energy, here is an exercise for you to do:

* Stand straight, with your feet flat on the floor and your arms held skyward. Clasp your hands together as far over your head as possible. Then, keeping your hands clasped, try to pull your hands apart. Strain to pull them apart while keeping them firmly clasped together. This steady, holding together is what Yang energy feels like.

* Again, stand straight with your feet flat on the floor, your arms held skyward, and your hands clasped together as far over your head as possible. This time, however, when you try to separate your clasped hands, allow them to slip apart. This is Yin energy. It is that which was once together but is now pulled apart; it yields.

In the classic sense, sexual energies are defined according to principle and polarity:

Yang Energy
The undivided ego—which seeks ever to divide. Objective, mental, self-confident, firm, analytical, assertive. Positive energy charge, descending current (from outside in). Carries within it the potential for Yin. Symbolically considered masculine. Straight (usually vertical) vision line within the inner eye.

Yin Energy
The divided ego—which seeks ever to unite. Subjective, emotional, compassionate, yielding, intuitive, passive. Negative energy charge, ascending current (from inside out). Carries within it the potential for Yang. Symbolically considered feminine. Curved (usually horizontal) vision line within the inner eye.

Also in the classic sense, orgasms and enlightenment (lesser and greater ecstasy) demonstrate how polarities of energy combine:

Orgasm
The ego merges with self—union, the pleasure of released energies, access to undifferentiated power. Scattered charge from either or both currents. Temporary satisfaction. Symbolically considered a physical bonding. Multi-directional (often spiraling) vision line within the inner eye.

Enlightenment
The ego-self reunifies with the Greater Self—convergence, reunion, pure ecstasy. Transcends the realms of energy; access to the omnipotent power of God. Ascending and descending currents meet with equal force, creating a light flash. Lasting satisfaction. Symbolically considered a spiritual transformation. All encompassing vision line, transcending the inner eye.

The reality of sexual energies and the experience of orgasm

helped ancient peoples to define and understand life processes and creation itself. Enlightenment was seen as the ultimate orgasm, whereby an individual surrendered to and was overwhelmed by a power greater than anything from the sensory world. This power was said to free individuals from earthplane attachments and introduce them to the truth of real knowledge and real power—an experience of God. Since enlightenment transfigures and transforms so visibly, people who experienced it were often revered as wise ones and chosen for leadership, guidance, or counseling roles.

5. MIND DEVELOPMENT

Rune use reflects whatever level of mind development and maturity you have attained. This is also true of other forms of divination. Here are some examples of the ways divination can be viewed by those of various mindsets:

> If you are selfish or vengeful, the guidance you seek can be manipulative or controlling, and trick you into thinking you are more powerful than you really are.
>
> If you are still childish in your reasoning, your interpretations can tend to be overly literal and rigid.
>
> Should play be your only interest in divination— the fun of a unique hobby—the guidance received is often unreliable or nonsensical.
>
> If you are excessively mechanistic or analytical, divinatory tools will have little value to you, and will seem to be a confusing array of practices "designed to cheat and enslave the unsuspecting."
>
> Should religious fundamentalism be your passion, divination will appear to be "the devil's work" and a sure-fire path to damnation—until you reread the Christian Bible and discover that, besides warnings against the misuse of such skills, this sacred text also contains a veritable digest of divination at its best.
>
> To the psychic, one divination skill can appear the same as another, valuable only as "proof" of psychic competence.

For the openly curious yet more mature, divination often becomes a way of reflecting back to the inner self whatever is being projected—of creating a psychological portrait helpful for inner growth.

With those who have developed an understanding of spirituality, divination will indeed signal "divinity" in the way it accesses more expansive realms of mind and spirit, and in the way it fosters respect for the sacredness of all lifeforms.

But for the mystic, ceremonies, rituals, objects, and tools cease to have much, if any, value. Gnosis (Knowing) surfaces for these people, enabling them to have more direct contact with whatever guidance or information might be helpful. Divinatory methods may seem unnecessary to them, or perhaps like an old "toy" long since discarded.

Divination can and will be whatever you make of it. As the simple tool it is, access is its only function, information is its only result. The tool of divination makes no difference in and of itself, for the attitude and the personal preference of the one who uses the tool determines its validity.

The more you understand yourself, the better you can appreciate others. The more at peace and confident you become, the more you have to share. Knowledge helps, but wisdom is better, for no matter how studied and experienced you are, true wisdom surfaces only when you have integrated on a cellular level what you think you know.

6. PSYCHIC POSSESSION

It is possible for a disembodied being or an energy mass to gain entry to and control of your body for periods of time seemingly without your permission. This is called "psychic possession." Don't tolerate this invasion. No ghostly being, thoughtform, or other "thing" has the right to invade your privacy and your life without permission. Just because a disincarnate or disembodied being might claim to be your guide or friend or an emissary from "higher" realms of spirit doesn't mean you are being told the truth. A disincarnate—someone who is dead (without a body)—or a spirit form can claim anything. These disincarnates, and lower astral beings (negative thoughtforms or spirits still attached to the earthplane), are quite real, but more of a nuisance than a threat. They can tempt you, proposition you, seem friendly enough, provide accurate guidance for awhile, make you feel important or needed—all for the purpose of cajoling you into letting them stick around. If you are lonely, feeling impotent or guilty, lost or unloved, needful of more attention and personal power, or perhaps on drugs or alcohol, the "deal" they offer may seem too good to refuse. *Just say no!*

Possession by another entity or energy form denies you your own free will. It is not worth the price of any promise.

Possession eventually drains vital energy from the host body and destroys both health and safety.

Negative energy feeds lower astral forms, allowing them to grow more powerful. Positive energy either dissolves these astral forms into nothingness or renders them powerless. You are not at their mercy, nor are you their victim. You have the power to take charge. It is your life and you are in control. Not everyone who alters their consciousness faces the prospect of possession, but, if you do, here are a few steps you can take:

* Do not allow yourself to feel or express any negative emotions when the "being" is present, for negativity can betray you or weaken your strength. Remember, you are in charge. Think positively. You have nothing to fear.

* Assert yourself and state your right to exist free of interference from anyone or anything from other levels of existence at any time.

* Affirm your identify as a child of God. You are protected by God. You are divine and whole and filled with God's holy light. Know this. Positively know this! See the light filling your entire being and surrounding you in a bubble of protective love.

* Command the spirit being, disincarnate, thought-

form, or whatever to be gone at once—totally gone, permanently gone, now!

* See the "being" disappear into the radiance of God's light. Know that this is true. Feel it. Affirm it.

* State that you are free, and that the air is clear and cleansed. Know there is only life and love and joy because there is only God. Nothing and no one can violate this truth. Affirm divine order.

Sometimes, problems with psychic possession are more the result of poor diet or lack of self-esteem than of any invasion by disincarnates or energy forms. It may not be the dead who should concern you but, rather, the way you live your life. Have a good health checkup. Pay special attention to your vitamin/mineral intake, your hormone balance, regular exercise, and the consumption of complete proteins. Make certain you are assimilating what you ingest, and take steps to strengthen your immune system. Healthy, happy people with positive self-images virtually never have problems with possession.

7. CHANNELING

The type of channeling that is popular today was once referred to as "trance mediumship." Trance mediumship involves an individual inviting, then allowing, a disembodied spirit being or entity to use his or her body, for the purpose of communicating with people still on the earthplane. This arrangement is based on temporary or occasional usage, and is agreed upon by all parties concerned. Various levels of the trance state can be employed, and numerous dimensions or realms of involvement can be reached. As is always true of any endeavor, mediumship—whether in trance or not—can be positive, negative, or a little of both. More often than not, it is usually the result of either the ego self or the Greater Self overshadowing the individual's personality. Even if a disincarnate, spirit guide, or transcendent entity should make contact, what then flows forth from the medium or channeler is seldom anything other than what could have been gained through the time-honored practices of meditation and prayer.

Originally, what we now call channeling was used as a means to contact the dead and prove there is life after death. Such channeled contacts did indeed produce provocative information, some of which was later verified. For example, the entire Xerox photocopy technique was credited by its inventor, Chester F. Carlson, as having come from spirit beings channeled through a trance medium.

Real channeling, however, covers far more than an emergence or manifestation of disincarnates. Channeling ability can signal mind-to-mind telepathy, including telepathy with animals; contact with other forms of intelligence such as elements, minerals, and plants; a visit from the proverbial Greek muses who, as legend tells us, inspire, motivate, and tease us into peaks of creativity and flashes of insight; and the influence of thoughtforms, your own or from others, as we digest and process various types of input.

If voices or thoughts other than your own seek your attention or try to come through you, use the following chart comparing energies from different levels as a guide before you decide to accept or reject what is happening:

LESSER MIND *The Voice of Ego* *Personality Level*	GREATER MIND *The Voice of Spirit* *Soul Level*
flatters	informs
commands	suggests
demands	guides
tests	nudges
chooses for you	leaves choice to you
imprisons	empowers
promotes dependency	promotes independence
intrudes	respects
pushes	supports
excludes	includes
is status oriented	is free and open

LESSER MIND	GREATER MIND
The Voice of Ego	*The Voice of Spirit*
Personality Level	*Soul Level*
insists on obedience	encourages growth and development
often claims ultimate authority	recognizes a greater power, or God
offers short-cuts	offers integration
seeks personal gratification	affirms divine order along with the good of the whole

Remember, whatever you project returns to you. Channeling information from another source does *not* exempt you from taking responsibility for the information that is delivered.

And especially remember: anyone who claims to be the only source of a spiritual revelation is either a fool or a fake. Channeling is a route through which anything can pass, and that's all it is. There are no guarantees in its use.

8. FORTUNE TELLING AND THE ISSUE OF POWER

Fortune telling—predicting what will definitely happen in the future—is impossible if divinatory tools are used properly. Probabilities can be surmised, but little else. The true purpose of divination is to seek and gain information from a broader perspective, which involves detaching oneself from the given situation and any emotional investment in its outcome. Divination involves relaxing, releasing ego needs, and surrendering to a higher or more expansive state of consciousness. These steps are necessary because the answer to any question always resides within the question itself, but at the next level up in vibration.

Information gained through divination offers objective viewpoints, not absolutes. The future is not as fixed as some people wish to think. Every time a new choice is made, the future changes and all the players on the stage of life shift positions. But, the goal of our particular life, our purpose for being here, does seem to be unchangeable. It is how we achieve our goal or fail in our effort that is entirely flexible. Free will, then, is the guarantee and the birthright of every soul to express. Even if we seem unable to change life's circumstances, we can always change our response to those circumstances. And changing our response eventually has a way of changing circumstances. Telling someone that a specific event will definitely occur programs that individual for the event to happen. And no one has the right to program another person. We can influence each other. We can teach, lead, guide, inspire, and motivate. But we cannot rob others of their power, their power of free will. Since what is given out returns, to enslave another is to enslave yourself; to manipulate or try to control another is to weaken your own power base.

Accurate predictions are often more indicative of how easy it is to program people than they are proof of any fortune teller's skill.

Fortune telling is wrapped up in the issue of power—what it is and how it is handled. The word "power" is derived from the Latin word for "to be able" and refers to every person's right to claim identity, recognition, and worthiness. True power inspires rather than forces, gives examples not orders, guides not directs, motivates not limits, and empowers not imprisons. True power is a gentle, magnetic radiance that is ever-expanding, ever-including, ever-uplifting. It is the harmonic balance between our inner and outer worlds—the activity of love.

9. SENSITIVITY AND BALANCE

Free-form rune casting is one of the most delightful methods I know for developing and learning to trust your own intuitive and psychic ability. It is immediate, demonstrative, and open-ended, thus providing an easy way to gauge progress and improvement. Other forms of divination offer some of these benefits, but not all of them. With this form of rune casting, the subconscious mind, and perhaps even the superconscious mind, can be more readily accessed. Traditionally, it is said that the mind consists of conscious, subconscious, and superconscious levels. Here is how I define these levels:

The Conscious Level feels wide-awake and alert. It collects and interprets facts and details from objective reality. It is associated with the left hemisphere of the brain.

The Subconscious Level feels dreamy and detached. It sifts and intuits creative possibilities from subjective reality. It is associated with the right hemisphere of the brain.

The Superconscious Level feels wise and knowing, as if it is connected to larger expanses of mind such as group, race, or universal mind. It infuses guidance from collective reality. It is associated with the limbic system of the brain.

There is nothing mystical, religious, or even fearsome about altering one's state of consciousness. We do it all the time whether we realize it or not. Altering consciousness is a natural process, and divination is based upon this fact. Psychism represents a vast world of mystery for most people, as it envelops the subtle energies of subjective reality. Psychic abilities allow us to enter this "other" world and look around. Psychic skills operate like antennae, extending the natural reach of faculties which are normal to us.

It has been my experience that, although psychism appears as different abilities and manifestations, it is really various expressions of the same mechanism, which can be controlled and trained. It is like a basic talent which can be directed into numerous channels. Call it a skill if you will. Just as with any other skill, it can be ignored, used as it is, or developed and improved with practice. It can also emerge seemingly full-blown at birth. Quite simply put, to be alive is to be psychic. Psychic ability is more akin to breathing than it is to riding a broomstick, despite popular attitudes. But, as with everything else in life, *use determines value.* Self-discipline makes a difference, and so does focus—because wherever you put your attention is where you put your power! By focusing on such attributes as the greater good, divine order, and wholeness, you can insure the healthy development of psychism. And by focusing on God, all levels of life automatically begin to balance in ways that are best for the highest good of all concerned.

Native Americans say, "Walk in balance," because they

recognize that balance (the integration of our physical, mental, emotional, and spiritual selves) is the secret of a life well lived. It is not who we are that matters, but what we have become; not what we possess, but what we have shared or given away. The bottom line is not profit, but service *plus* long-term investment in the education and upliftment of others.

✷

It is my hope that this material on cautions proves helpful to you, and provides a sound base from which to determine for yourself what has value and what doesn't. The realms of spirit are not frightful, and the depths of divination need not be mysterious. When we practice divinatory skills, we are really exploring our own capacities and potentials to stretch beyond our apparent limitations. In a very real sense, divination is a form of "spiritual calisthenics."

As a final note, the words "magic," "magnet," and "magnetic" were all derived from the Babylonian and Persian word *magno*, which means "receptive." Think about that.

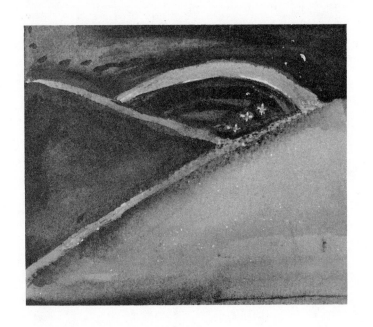

6
memories &
the mind

While I was researching the darkened depths of time for what might be the spawning ground of runes, I uncovered more than I bargained for. Modern technology and a new breed of highly skilled professionals have turned upside down the knowledge of ancient times, and have rendered as fiction some of what was once thought to be fact. As today's inquisitive minds access more material and recheck former findings, the puzzle pieces of the past have begun to fit a different mold—one that is far more fascinating and far more thought-provoking than previously believed possible.

Certainly this is a book about runes and divination, not a book about history per se, but, if you will bear with me, I think you will find the following brief excursion into times past quite worth taking. And, in a strange way, this excursion may help to clarify why so many people recognize runic glyphs as if the glyphs were part of their own personal memories. By looking backward we can better understand the present, and maybe even how life itself evolves.

Consider that geoscientists using acoustic waves generated by earthquakes have produced scans which show remnants of continents and other structures in and near the earth's core. Also consider that recent satellite photographs reveal surface features on earth indicative of advanced civilizations so old that no records exist to clearly identify them.

New dating techniques have created an embarrassing abundance of artifacts that defy previous scholarship. There are acid batteries over 2,000 years old; electricity in battery form going back to the Sumerian culture; the common use of aluminum in fourth-century Chinese art; iron milling (covering iron with silicon) thousands of years old; modern-looking human skulls 100,000 years old; a sparkplug encased in rock dating back 500,000 years; and a sandal print of a right foot stepping on trilobites over six million years ago.

Such anomalies nullify the idea of a progressive linear history, evidencing instead sweeping cycles of brilliant ascension followed by catastrophic decline. And as one anonymous archaeologist noted, "Always there are Noahs—survivors to see the next cycle."

Among "primitive" remnants still existing we have the Great Pyramid at Giza, from which the earth's size and shape can be calculated, including the degree of equatorial bulge and polar flatness, to a precision matched only by today's satellite measurements. Popular opinion dates the Pyramid at around 3,000 B.C., but most professionals feel that this date is still imprecise. So how old is it? And who built it, and why? Even today, we could not duplicate this architectural feat.

Then we have a most unusual poem, an epic of ancient India called the "Mahabharata." The world's longest poetic masterpiece, it consists of 100,000 stanzas. Although parts of the poem can be traced to 3,102 B.C., its oral traditions are claimed to stem from 10,000 years ago. In the last of its three major sections, it describes what was probably a nuclear holocaust, complete with the dropping of bombs from airborne craft, mushroom clouds, scorched earth, and vaporized people and animals. Of two sites bombed by the "Rods of Brahmin" in this poem, one of them, the south-central Deccan Valley, still today exhibits evidence of vitrification (surface melt from sudden extreme heat) and harbors bones which have been found to register radiation fifty times above levels normal for that area. A huge mountain of glass in the Brazilian jungle is said to have resulted from that same holocaust, which supposedly wiped out many ancient cities and the lost continent of Atlantis, as well.

Could Nagasaki and Hiroshima be repeats of a far more ancient folly? Recorded in what we know of history are endless examples of such catastrophic destruction. Legends and myths

from every culture on earth describe the rise of advanced societies and their devastating declines which swept away all traces of
their existence, save for a few struggling survivors. Nothing
remains but memories and the telling of tales.

It has been my experience that history only repeats itself
when people fail to learn from it, yet the cycles referred to here
cover time periods so vast that one wonders how learning
accumulation can occur when knowledge to support that learning does not remain constant. Yet evidence suggests another
possibility: could we as intelligent beings have forgotten or
refused to honor another facet of our own intelligence? It seems
to me that we have brushed aside our *memories!*

Persisting in the modern psyche of humanity are dreams
and visions of other lives, other worlds, other civilizations, other
times—all so strikingly similar that childhood fantasies, cultural
traditions, and even reincarnational memories do not fully
explain them away.

In the book, *The Letters of J.R.R. Tolkien,* edited by Humphrey Carpenter with the assistance of Christopher Tolkien,
there are various passages which reveal some surprising things
about J.R.R. Tolkien and what propelled him to produce his
many books on Middle Earth, which are one of the greatest
treasures of fantasy/myth ever undertaken. Tolkien said:

> Yet always I had the sense of recording what was already
> 'there'. . .that I was not inventing but reporting. . . .For
> when Faramir speaks of his private vision of the Great
> Wave, he speaks for me. That vision and dream has been
> ever with me. . . .What I might call my Atlantis-haunting.
> This legend or myth or dim memory of some ancient his-
> tory has always troubled me. In sleep I had the dreadful
> dream of the ineluctable Wave, either coming out of the
> quiet sea, or coming in towering over the green inlands. It
> still occurs occasionally, though now exorcized by writing
> about it. It always ends by surrender, and I awake gasping
> out of deep water. . . .I began an abortive book of time-
> travel of which the end was to be the presence of my hero
> in the drowning of Atlantis. This was to be called
> '*Numenor,' Land in the West*. . . .Though it is only in read-

ing the work myself (with criticisms in mind) that I become aware of the dominance of the theme of Death . . . that the 'message' was the hideous peril of confusing true 'immortality' with limitless serial longevity. Freedom from Time, and clinging to Time.

✳

Surely there must exist somewhere, somehow, a kind of "central storage bank" of collective memory—invisible, etheric, and accessible subconsciously or consciously—which contains imprints and impressions from all that was, all that is, and, perhaps, all that might ever be. Freud labeled this possible storage bank "racial memory" and Jung called it "the collective unconscious." Metaphysically, it is often referred to as "universal mind," or "mass mind," or the "Akashic records." However labeled, it seems to be a "place" or perhaps a "field" where group memories and various kinds of information are stored.

Recognizing and investigating the validity of information from this memory source is as important to the understanding of history and human development as the procurement and study of physical evidence. *Neither source of information is complete without the other.*

Other archetypal reservoirs of memory may also exist, layers of them, each for different reasons and different purposes. We know, for instance, that molecular DNA ribbons direct the mechanics of physical reproduction, but what directs the DNA? Chemical interactions within DNA do not dictate evolution. So what does?

Rupert Sheldrake, an English plant biologist, has come up with what he feels is the answer, and that answer, described in his book, *A New Science of Life,* is well worth taking time to consider. Sheldrake theorizes that primary sources of mass memory do indeed exist, residing in non-energetic currents or fields which permeate existence. He names these "morphogenetic" (Greek for "form beginning") fields or "M-fields." According to Sheldrake, these M-fields direct the shape, development, and basic behavior of all living species and systems, functioning as invisible blueprints or connecting memories, if you will, linking any member of a given species or system with its fellows while supplying a ready bank of accumulated information that members can instinctively and automatically draw from or contribute to. M-fields, then, constantly change and evolve as individual members learn and grow. Changes in the field, however, are not always instantaneous. Sometimes a certain threshold must first be reached before the entire field is affected. Once the total number of changed individual members reaches that threshold, field activation occurs and all members, no matter where they are located or how much time has lapsed, are then stimulated to copy or express the change. Incredible as it seems, all attempts to disprove Sheldrake's bizarre theory have only added to the mountains of evidence supporting it.

A recent example of how Sheldrake believes M-fields work would be the situation in Europe regarding the small bird called the Blue Tit. This little warbler discovered how to open foil caps from milk bottles left on doorsteps and drink off the top cream. Once the Blue Tits within a small area had taught each other the trick and then mastered it, suddenly all the other Blue Tits across the entire European continent were doing the same thing without benefit of either direct exposure or teaching. The same thing happened with Macaca Fuscata monkeys on an island off the northern coast of Japan. One monkey discovered how to wash freshly dug sweet potatoes before eating them and then taught this to some other monkeys. Soon after most of the island monkeys had learned and mastered the new trick, all the other monkeys of that species on other islands and even on the mainland were doing it too. In both these cases, physical contact between the various species members was not possible, yet the new skills were transmitted to every member as if by "magic."

It is important to note here that human history is crammed with examples duplicating these found among animals—cases where ideas and skills have spread to far-flung corners of the globe without physical evidence to support how such information was communicated. Because of new dating procedures, we now know that the possibility of one human culture physically influencing another is different than previously believed.

Consider these puzzles. Sumerians and Babylonians "suddenly" started practicing advanced astronomy and geometry *after* mysterious builders of northern European passage graves *had already* developed and perfected both sciences. Romans erected aqueducts and complex irrigation and plumbing systems *after* these were in wide use by Mayans on the opposite side of the globe. Yoga postures were *routinely* practiced from southern Russia to northern Europe *before* being "invented" in India. Trial by jury and democratic codes of law were *common* in many areas of deepest Africa *before* "civilized" empires in Asia and Europe "originated" such ideas. Rituals and priesthood practices of Celtic Druids *paralleled* those of Hindu Brahmans. Nearly identical megalithic stone monuments "suddenly" sprang up throughout coastal Europe, the British Isles, northern Africa, and the Pacific *long before* Phoenician sailors explored the seas, supposedly spreading such ideas and culture as they went. Stone-circle worship centers are almost identical no matter where in the world they are found, from England to Peru, from Polynesia to the State of Wyoming. What seemed to be the birth of the Golden Age of Reason around 500 B.C. (when Buddha, Pythagoras, Confucius, and Lao-Tzu lived, and the secular use of runes began) was actually *a spontaneous global rediscovery and redefinition of knowledge that was already ancient.*

As if these puzzles were not enough to think about, here are a few more. Names and games are almost identical throughout the world. Children's stories are equally similar, with over 300 versions of "Cinderella" known to exist. There is the "Kalevala," a Finnish compilation of ancient mystical folk tales concerning creation, chivalry, heroism, and common life; and there is the "Kabbala," a Jewish compilation of ancient mystical interpretations of scripture emphasizing the nearness of God for everyone. The Tree of Life is central to both works, as is the message of God's importance in daily living. In fact, the Tree of Life is central to many different spiritual and religious groups and was in use *long before* the coming of Christianity *or* Judaism.

How did all this happen? By accident? Did UFOs zoom

around seeding people's minds? Or did early inhabitants understand flight and have airborne craft?

Although some evidence exists indicating the possibility of intergalactic visitors and ancient airplanes, it is often not taken seriously. Most people simply settle for the idea of "coincidence" or the fact that similar problems are solved by similar solutions. None of these ideas, however, adequately addresses the amazing scope and consistency of plagiarism and cultural copying which was and still is globally rampant.

Even Indiana Jones, hero of the modern movie favorite, "Indiana Jones and the Raiders of the Lost Ark," seems to be a hyped-up version of another adventurous archaeologist, Inigo Jones, who, in the 1600s, was commissioned by King Charles I of England to probe the mysteries of Stonehenge. Any invention you can name was invented at approximately the same time by a number of different people, each working independently and often unaware of the others' work. Invention credits have always been decided by who received recognition first rather than who invented first! Magazine editors almost routinely deal with *spontaneous* repetitive submissions on the same subject, even if it is fiction. Unintentional copying occurs in every creative medium from music to math.

As an old adage reminds us, "Once it is done by one it is done for all."

Sheldrake continues his theory by explaining that M-fields evolve. They are not static. Indeed, *no* layer of *any* kind of memory is static. Every thought, word, and deed, everything seen, heard, felt, or sensed, is stored away in some kind of memory storage bank, and each contribution to that storage bank either expands or diminishes the accumulated inventory. These invisible, floating "libraries" are accessible through the subconscious during moments of passive relaxation, intense concentration, or accelerated activity. We often enter and exit a full range of such "libraries" when we play, dream, imagine, wonder, muse, intuit, invent, experiment, read, reflect, meditate, create, compete, fantasize, focus, study, exercise, labor, run, trance out, and so forth. Whenever we completely lose ourselves in what we are doing, whenever we focus or unfocus to the point that all which is extraneous disappears, we automatically access memory and the depths of mass mind. And we can alter or change whatever we find there.

Plato said, "All knowledge is recollection," implying that we learn only that which we already know or are in harmony with.

Science tells us that it takes only one-tenth of one percent of a group of light waves to influence all the other light waves to follow them and create a pattern of coherence. If you swing one suspended steel beam in a room full of steel beams, soon all of them will be swinging in unison with the first. Women living together eventually experience their menses at the same time. Public trends in the marketplace and on Wall Street follow similar patterns. Is the threshold ratio of light waves also the threshold ratio for Sheldrake's M-fields and the human body and the collective mind and, for that matter, all forms of intelligence and matter itself?

Considering that science also tells us that matter is simply solidified light, we might reconsider resonance. Resonance is a stable condition caused by correlations between rhythm and coherence (the synchronicity of relationships in motion). It is an oscillating field array which adheres to an overall pattern. This might account for the way memories work, for how one mind can affect all minds, and for how history—all history—is remembered.

Simon Henderson, writing in the Fall 1987 issue of *Wildfire* magazine, notes that there are two kinds of learning: symbol and pattern. He says individuals in pattern-literate societies have highly accurate recall of a vast array of knowledge, whereas individuals in symbol-literate societies require massive and elaborate materials storage—such as with books, computers, libraries, and files. Symbol learning utilizes character representations like letters and numbers, while pattern learning utilizes muscle memory and harmonic memory.

> Pattern knowledge that was passed on from one generation to the next is known as muscle memory (in dance) and harmonic memory (in song)—both of which are highly accurate in time. The sun verse of the Anasazi (for instance) was sung to a .001 second's accuracy each time,

which is more accurate than most stopwatches. The time was remembered in their muscle movement and it was remembered in the song—and those that forgot could be reminded by others of the tribe, as all people shared this knowledge. The harmonic memory was also inherent in the art, which was not art as we understand it, but a sophisticated, scientific record of the common knowledge to which thousands of generations of people had added and amended information as new knowledge evolved.

There are West African tribes utilizing pattern oral knowledge in Nigeria who can chant back the combined knowledge of 1,600 to 2,000 generations, which traces back much further than the Bible. Traditional people in isolated islands in the South Pacific can still accurately navigate to over 1,500 islands using the same navigational patterns taught them by their ancestors.

Henderson went on to point out:

In contrasting the strengths of pattern-literate societies with our contemporary society we see that we produce individuals with university degrees that remember relatively little of what they have learned. Our civilization, rather than sharing in common knowledge, has produced such a wide diversity of specialized knowledge that we often feel isolated from one another.

The basics of Henderson's ideas are similar to the writings of Jean M. Auel in her Earth Children Series. Using the time frame of 35,000 to 20,000 B.C., she weaves a compelling story of one woman's life and of what actually could have happened during that period in history based on today's latest research findings. She also vividly describes the dream worlds of these early people, and the importance of collective memories as a major source of information, knowledge, and truth.

The dream concept Auel advances is not that different from the "dreamtime" concept of the Australian aborigines. The aborigines believe that two worlds exist, not just one: waketime and dreamtime. Each of these worlds is equally solid, real, active, and dynamic. According to the aboriginal belief, dreamtime can be entered a number of ways: while asleep, by conscious will, through merging and joining, or because of a trance induced by sound, movement, or ingested substances. Once entered, dreamtime is said to operate slightly in advance of wake time, thus allowing "second sight" and the ability to become one with any person, place, or thing. Aborigines engaged in "dreaming" (the act of transferring consciousness from wake time to dreamtime) are renowned for their ability to "see" hundreds and sometimes thousands of miles away and to accurately report not only what they observe but also what they hear, feel, and smell. They prophesy in this state, and psychically intercede in cases where assistance can be given. The knowledge they gain from their version of dreaming is phenomenal in its precise and verifiable detail. Using modern terminology, it could be said that their beliefs actually describe two separate but parallel time/space continua with one flowing somewhat ahead of the other. Random travel between these worlds is common, but specific journeys can be directed by conscious control.

The kind of memory reached from dream depths is primordial in power and strength, yet we relegate it to symbolic myth in "civilized" society. Aboriginal dreaming is little different, really, from any other type of mind or spirit projection used by native peoples. What is often mistakenly classified as uncivilized or pagan behavior is in reality a trust in inner guidance and an acknowledgement of the sacredness and validity of memory.

If we are to ever understand the roots of our own being, we must first come to recognize that the psychic reality of dream life is as valid and important as the physical reality of waking existence.

Dreams and visions are the playground of the subconscious and a springboard to layers of memory. They are pathways to unlimited reserves of information and wisdom. You don't have to be asleep to experience them, nor is their content always relegated to the past.

By moving in and through dream depths, *consciously or subconsciously,* we can glimpse ancient memories of how images were formed and patterns took shape, of how behaviors were repeated into habits, and of how survival needs became so powerful that we have yet to satisfy them today, tens of thousands of years later. We meet our own beginnings in this memory dream-pool, our accumulated histories and possible futures, plus the reasons behind almost everything we do. All pathways sooner or later lead into this never-never-land of the mind, so universal yet so intimate and personal. It is the doorway to our Source.

We are each the summation of countless millenia and untold rebirthings. Life does not so much graduate its members as it celebrates with them the continual rise of new beginnings.

No one can possess universal mind. It can be accessed by all but belongs to none. Only temporal claim can we make to that small portion which is filtered and enhanced through our individual brains. Mind itself remains forever elusive and mysterious, even on this edge of the twenty-first century. But mind can be traveled and it can be used. We can harness endless potentials from the limitless range of its power.

One mind, many thinkers.

Because there is only one mind, each of us has a vested interest in the existence and growth of all other beingness. We are connected—you, I, all living things, and every level of intelligence. What happens to one of us somehow affects us all, just as the trembling of a daisy touches the farthest star.

Some people say that it is reincarnational memories which surface with rune use. Perhaps so. And yet anyone can remember runes, even to a surprising degree. Certainly many of us have been personally affected by runes during various sojourns (lifetimes) we have taken in the earthplane, but over a decade of teaching runic secrets to others has convinced me that the child-like simplicity of the glyphs is what allows the collective mind to be tapped by anyone who wishes to do so. People remember runes because, at some incredible level of mind, all memory is held in common and nothing is forgotten.

The art of divination enables us to stop time, isolate a given moment, study its characteristics, discover its potential, and then compare our findings with their precedent from the realms of memory. This process takes only an instant, because an instant is the only time we really have.

History is cyclic. Civilizations come and go. Humanity learns and evolves and grows. But the mind continually encompasses and envelops all that exists as if it were somehow an entity of its own—pure consciousness aware of itself.

As our space travelers have proven that there are no boundaries upon earth, so our spirit travelers have shown us that there are no boundaries within the mind.

7
language
of spirit

Any historical documentation of runes, as well as any attempt to justify their use or meaning, not only falls short but utterly fails to capture what they really are—for runes are not as they seem. Their use in written language occurred far later in time than their use as a divination system. Even the ritualized glyphs are comparatively young when viewed from the perspective of image making and the beginnings of creative thought and collective memories.

Runes, though they were not always called such, go back tens of thousands of years. Their history defies clear tracking, except through the few ancient paintings and carvings which survive, taunting us, and puzzling sleuths who would call themselves professionals.

But real runes, true runes, are the *patterns* formed from unwritten images, patterns which comprise pictures that pull at the heartstrings and snuggle deep within the mind. The physical, carved, or written glyphs are but refined attempts to organize and record these runes, making the truisms they convey more available and more practical to more people. There are countless systems of glyphs. Some of these systems are local, some regional, and some widespread. They exist for almost every use imaginable. But the runes, the runes themselves— well, they are another story.

Let us take a step beyond history and beyond all languages which have ever come to be. Let us take a step beyond even myth and legend, for there is yet more to discover of runes.

To better understand what we seek, let us be reminded of

other ancient texts, of songs and stories which refer to runic magic as *lays* (short poems of deep meaning which are sung) and as *vignettes* (short stories filled with mystical mysteries which evoke emotional response). Let us also remember that runes refer to the artistic ability to contour pebble-like shapes into smooth mounds with rough angular markings. Remembering this, let us go backward in time once again to view our primordial beginnings.

Long before there was ever a need or desire for tangible records, there was a desire and passion for recreating patterns in the mind which would evoke the immediacy of special moments. These special moments were ones filled with awe and wonder. They were moments when earth and sky, heaven and human, seemed to merge, intermingling the visible with the invisible. Such would have been moments when spirit reigned.

These patterns in the mind would have quickly become anchored in collective memory because of their connection to basic comprehension and survival itself. Once fixed in memory, they would have become instinctual, and our response to them emotional.

These patterns in the mind are runes.

Runes are not just any kind of thought pattern. They are unique arrangements of shape and form which show us what to reach for and what to reject in our lives and in our environment. They are like subliminal survival symbols so powerfully entrenched within us that they seem to live and breathe with a life of their own.

Real runes are the purest of magic and mystery, for, once aroused or stimulated, they bring to mind special moments suspended in time, moments connected to nature and everything which is natural. Real runes are beyond what words can tell, for they are affairs of the heart and messengers of the soul. We know them. We cannot forget them. No one can. They are too deeply embedded within our depths. We know them on a gut level, not a thinking level. We respond to them without knowing why. We understand them without any sense of logic. No one can really learn of runes because none of us ever forgot them in the first place.

They strum the chords of our deepest memories. They are the "kisses" which life gives itself.

To regard runes only as glyphs engraved on objects is to lose forever their true meaning. Glyphs are but representative designs — runes are living passion!

Of all the people who have written about runes, I know of only one individual of modern vintage who even comes close to stroking their secrets. Using the format of vignettes, he delved as deep as words can deliver into the heart and soul of runes. His name was Sigurd F. Olson, and he was well known in his time as an avid ecologist and interpretive naturalist who dedicated his life to the understanding and preservation of wilderness. Sigurd was well-educated, a professor and dean, the recipient of many awards and honorary degrees, a past president of the Wilderness Society and National Parks Association, as well as a consultant to the U.S. Department of the Interior. He left this life in 1982, departing from his home in Ely, Minnesota, gateway to the wilds he came to know so well as a guide in his youth.

Sigurd was familiar with the "Kalevala" and understood its runic lays. He knew Nordic and Finnish history well and the myths of old. Among his many books was the simple yet eloquent, *Runes of the North*. Its publisher, Alfred A. Knopf, New York, has granted me permission to quote some passages at random. Although out of context, these brief glimpses will at least give you a "taste" and "feel" for what I believe runes really are.

Tall aspen stand among the cedars surrounding the cabin, and as the wind blows they whisper an ancient song. Along the ridge protecting it from the north, are birches growing among the rocks, clusters of striped maple, and hazel. Chickadees and nuthatches are around my sauna cabin, and in one of the tallest trees, pileated woodpeckers have built their nest.

A flying squirrel lives in a hole under the roof and, when it comes out, it spreads its legs and sails to the nearest balsam. I saw it the other night and its eyes were liquid and black, its fur a greyish tan and softer than chinchilla, its wing strips edged with sable. A beautiful creature, I am glad it has taken its abode in so important a place as my sauna.

Along the trail to the lake are huge stones with depressions between them reaching down to the dark, wet roots of the cedar. The boulders are covered with sphagnum and in it grow gold thread, violets, and strange fungi. All these living things are part of the sauna cabin, as they are part of the woods and rocks around it. It is a place of delight and beauty woven into the experience itself.

Over the lake lay a sense of impending doom and we make everything safe: canoes well up among the trees, tent stakes reinforced, ropes so tight they sang when we touched them. All we owned was covered: food, equipment, dry wood under tarpaulins weighted down with heavy stones. We were at the shore ready to fly for the tent the instant the wind and deluge came.

Then a strange and eerie light was over the lake and the surrounding hills, a greenish-yellow glow that was almost tarnished gold. Rushes once black were illumined now, leaned like silver rapiers as the air began to move. The stump became alive, lost its jagged contours, and was a thing of beauty against the opalescence of the water. The cliffs and pines against the channel turned to burnished copper. Then came the wind and the rain in a final crashing rumble—and the glory was gone.

My little dream net spoke of many things to me, of love for children, of tolerance and the intangible qualities which give warmth and meaning to life. When I accepted it, I did so with humility because for me it was a symbol not only of trust and acceptance by my Indian friend, but a hint of the long past and a world of dreams most moderns have forgotten.

Not long ago I slept under a pine tree with my six-year-old grandson Derek. We had a tiny fire and lay in our sleeping bags watching the reflection of dying embers against the branches and how it turned them to gold and bronze and copper. I told him many stories of moose and bear and, at the end, the legend of the dream net; he believed, for he was young and still had faith. Above us that night was the ancient net, and the night was full of dreams both good and bad. He could see them, feel them, and when I told him that only the good ones came through, he closed his eyes quietly and went to sleep.

If you have never read *Runes of the North* by Sigurd F. Olson, do so. It is a gem. The book has recently been reprinted, but is also available through most libraries.

Sigurd writes as well as anyone can of real runes, those patterns of thought formed by our emotional response to moments uniquely special, yet common to us all. But these runes, true runes, are beyond the reach of words—for they are *the language of spirit.*

It has been my purpose in writing this book to pass along a wondrous gift which was once given me. I have shared what these paper pages can hold. The rest, like the underside of an iceberg, awaits your greater discovery. Prepare yourself a set and begin your own journey through the depths of memories and the mind.

There are more to runes than I could ever say, for they are magic, and filled with the wonder of surprise.

RESOURCE SUGGESTIONS

Because I honor the divine right of each individual to pursue his or her own path toward truth, my books always include a resource section. It is not meant as a comprehensive index but, rather, as a gesture of sharing some of the best sources and resources currently available. I cannot make any promises or guarantees about anything listed here, but I can offer these resources as a place to begin your search for additional information. It is my hope that you will find this material interesting, helpful, and, above all, challenging.

Enjoy.

RUNIC REFERENCES

The Book of Runes, by Ralph Blum. New York, NY; St. Martin's Press, 1982. Includes ceramic glyphs and pouch.

The New Book of Runes, by Ralph Blum. New York, NY; St. Martin's Press, 1987.

Futhark: A Handbook of Rune Magic, by Edred Thorsson. York Beach, ME; Weiser Books, 1984.

Runelore: A Handbook of Esoteric Runology, by Edred Thorsson. York Beach, ME; Weiser Books, 1986.

At the Well of Wyrd: A Handbook of Runic Divination, by Edred Thorsson. York Beach, ME; Weiser Books, 1988.

The Runic Workbook, by Tony Willis. London, England; Aquarian Press, 1986 (handled in the U.S. through Sterling Publishers, New York).

Rune Magic, by Donald Tyson. St. Paul, MN; Llewellyn Publishers, 1988.

Rune Magic and the separate *Rune Magic Set,* all by Deon Dolphin. San Bernardino, CA; Borgo Press, 1988. The set includes Celtic runestones, pouch, and casting cloth.

The Runes and Other Magical Alphabets, by Michael E. Howard. London, England; Aquarian Press, 1978 (handled in the U.S. through Sterling Publishers, New York).

The Secret of the Runes, by the German scholar Guido von List. Originally published in 1908. Edited and translated by Stephen Flowers, Ph.D. New York, NY; Destiny Books, 1988.

MacRune, a high-tech, high-touch computer software game put out by Macintosh. Available at any computer software outlet.

For those interested in an organizational network of people using various types of runes, a **Rune Guild** now exists to explore runic lore and wisdoms, and to help people get in touch with each other. Query for additional information. Write: Rune Guild, P.O. Box 7622, Austin, TX 78713.

You can find **pebbles** very much like the ones I have through various sources, among them gift shops, gemstone catalogues, flower-arranging boutiques, and some garden stores. Ask for **Japanese polished stones** used to anchor flower arrangements, or simply "stones by the pound." Many times you can find stores selling crystals and gemstones that are cut and tumbled to a perfect size for rune use. One garden catalogue which carries the Japanese flower-arranging stones is: Smith and Hawken Gardening Catalogue, 25 Corte Madera, Mill Valley, CA 94941; phone (415) 383-4050. A gift catalog which lists the right size of rose quartz and hematite can be obtained from The Nature Company, P.O. Box 2310, Berkeley, CA 94702; phone 1-800-227-1114. Naturally, if you can find your own stones out in the wilds they will mean more to you—and they will be more personal.

OTHER REFERENCES MADE IN THIS BOOK

Just So Stories, by Rudyard Kipling. New York, NY; Weathervane Books, 1978.

The Hobbit, or There and Back Again, by J.R.R. Tolkien. Boston, MA; Houghton Mifflin Company, 1984.

The Lord of the Rings, by J.R.R. Tolkien. Boston, MA; Houghton Mifflin Company, 1965.

The Silmarillion, by J.R.R. Tolkien. Boston, MA; Houghton Mifflin Company, 1977.

The Letters of J.R.R. Tolkien, selected and edited by Humphrey Carpenter, with the assistance of Christopher Tolkien. Boston, MA; Houghton Mifflin Company, 1981. (All these issues of Tolkien's books were originally published by George Allen and Unwin Publishers, Ltd.)

The Clan of the Cave Bear, by Jean M. Auel (of the Earth Children Series). New York, NY; Crown, 1980.

The Valley of Horses, by Jean M. Auel (of the Earth Children Series). New York, NY; Crown, 1982.

The Mammoth Hunters, by Jean M. Auel (of the Earth Children Series). New York, NY; Crown, 1985.

Runes of the North, by Sigurd F. Olson. New York, NY; Alfred A. Knopf, 1985.

Ogam, the Poet's Secret, by Sean O'Boyle and published by Gilbert Dalton. Available from Tranquil Things, Box 338, Derby Line, VT 05830.

Ogam, Consaine & Tifinag Alphabets—Ancient Uses, by Warren W. Dexter. Rutland, VT; Academy Books, 1984.

The Once and Future Star, by George Michanowsky. New York, NY; Hawthorn Books, 1977.

The Stars and the Stones, by Martin Brennan. London, England; Thames and Hudson, 1983.

America B.C., by Barry Fell. New York, NY; Pocket Books, 1976.

The Key, by John Philip Cohane. New York, NY; Crown, 1969.

Before Columbus: Links Between the Old World & Ancient America, by Cyrus Herzl Gordon. New York, NY; Crown, 1971.

Ancient Mysteries, Modern Visions, by Philip S. Callahan. Published in 1984 and available from Acres U.S.A., P.O. Box 9547, Kansas City, MO 64133.

The New View Over Atlantis, by John Michell. New York, NY; Harper & Row, 1983.

A New Science of Life: The Hypothesis of Formative Causation, by Rupert Sheldrake. Los Angeles, CA; J.P. Tarcher/Houghton Mifflin, 1981.

KALEVALA, POETIC & PROSE EDDA

Heroes of the Kalevala, by Babette Deutsch. New York, NY; Julian Messner, Inc., 1940.

Kansanruno-Kalevala, by Elias Lönnrot, edited by Matti Kuusi. Keuruu, Finland; Otava Publishing Co., 1977.

For more information about the Kalevala and other folklore, inquire through: The American Folklife Center, Library of Congress, Washington, DC, 20540; phone (202) 287-6590.

STORYTELLING

One of the ancient skills that is the most missed and needed today is the art of **storytelling**. Through its use, great truths and wisdoms were conveyed, along with proper codes of conduct and morals. I am happy to say that this wonderful artform and teaching tool is now undergoing a renaissance. For more information, write to: National Association for the Preservation and Perpetuation of Storytelling, P.O. Box 309, Jonesborough, TN 37659.

HUNA

The best way I know to introduce yourself to this philosophic yet incredibly practical religion of the Hawaiian Islands is through the organization called **Huna Research, Inc.** Founded and directed by Dr. E. Otha Wingo, it is dedicated to the preservation, dissemination, and offering of Huna writings, materials, teaching tools, and classes. The quote I carried in this book is

from the Autumn 1984 issue of *Huna Work International.*
Inquiries are always welcome. Contact: Huna Research, Inc.,
1760 Anna Street, Cape Girardeau, MO 63701; phone (314)
334-3478.

ANOMALIES

A good definition of "anomalies" can be found in *Mysteries of
the Unexplained,* which was published by *Reader's Digest* in
1982: "Any departure from the expected arrangement, general
rule, or usual method is considered to be an anomaly and, as
such, is dismissed as largely suspect by the scientific community." If you want a fascinating read, get the book. Brad Steiger
has written several books about anomalies also. The Fortean
Society specializes in it (contact them through INFO, P.O. Box
387, Arlington, VA 22210-0387).

WILDFIRE MAGAZINE

There is no other magazine anywhere which quite equals *Wildfire.* It combines Native American concerns, shamanism,
ecology, survival issues, poetry, art, and just plain common
sense to present a "something-for-everyone" format. *Wildfire* is
one of many projects from **The Bear Tribe Medicine Society,**
headed by Sun Bear, a Chippewa Medicine Man. Through The
Bear Tribe, a full range of offerings are available: a mail-order
catalog, classes in survival skills, vision quests, apprenticeship
training, spiritual renewal sessions, and Medicine Wheel
Gatherings held in different places across the United States and
Europe. To learn more about the magazine and the organization behind it, contact: The Bear Tribe, P.O. Box 9167, Spokane,
WA 99209; phone (509) 326-6561.

SOUNDS AND LANGUAGE

Numerous research findings are now available concerning how
the spoken sound of language actually molds and shapes the
human brain. This fact is extremely important and deserving of
more attention. It seems that most of the ancient languages
were designed to elicit specific energetic responses in body and
mind from each particular arrangement of tone, pitch, and
vibration. Sanskrit is an example. It was designed to activate

mass memory and spiritual recall through the stimulation of endocrine centers (chakras) and spinal energies (kundalini) and the skeletal and nervous systems. The real secret to its mystical messages is the way it is pronounced. Hawaiian is the same way. Languages, like runes, which were unspoken, work through eye contact, touch, emotional response, and intuition to activate memory.

Here are two books to consider on the **power of sound:**

Sound Health: The Music and Sounds That Make Us Whole, by Steven Halpern with Louis Savary. San Francisco, CA; Harper & Row, 1985.

The Secret Power of Music, by David Tame. New York NY; Destiny Books, 1984.

Thanks to the New Age, there is now an incredible range of worthwhile music available. Go to your nearest store which carries New Age music and browse. I would particularly like to call your attention to one type of music, called **hoomi singing.** Hoomi singing was said to have originated in Mongolia. It utilizes many parts of the human body, in addition to the vocal cords, to create overtones or a series of notes from a single tone. In this system, sound is refracted by the human body to duplicate sounds of nature and the cosmos. Musical instruments are seldom used. Because of a recent renaissance in this ancient skill, hoomi singing has made a comeback under the name **harmonic singing.** One group performing this way is David Hykes and the Harmonic Choir. Two of their albums are *Hearing Solar Winds* and *A Harmonic Meeting.* Should you have difficulty finding these, contact this distributor and ask where the nearest outlet store is in your neighborhood: Back Roads, 417 Tamal Plaza, Corte Madera, CA 94925; phone (415) 924-4848. Remember, Back Roads is a distributor, not a retail outlet. All they can give you is information. I mention this type of music for a special reason. Of all the music I have yet heard since reviving from three near-death episodes, hoomi (harmonic) singing is the closest to what I heard while on The Other Side. I admit my bias here, but I think you will also find this music most unique.

Before I leave the subject of sounds and music, I want to mention the *Serenity Tapes.* Produced by Jim Moeller to awaken the heart, this line of musical offerings is special. Many artists contributed their talents to make up the "Serenity" sound—people influenced by A *Course in Miracles* philosophy and / or a desire to recommit themselves to spirituality and sacredness. For a full listing of music available, contact: Serenity, 180 W. 25th Street, Upland, CA 91786-1113; phone (714) 981-2318, or call 1-800-869-1684.

ARCHAEOLOGY, ASTRO-ARCHAEOLOGY, AND EARTH ENERGY LINES

For information about the non-profit **teaching and research organization** dedicated to conserving evidence of humanity's history, write to Dorothy L. Hayden, Director of Membership, The American Institute for Archaeological Research, Inc., 24 Cross Road, Mt. Vernon, NH 03057.

The **Gungywamp Society,** composed primarily of interested lay people who are curious about the connections between earth mysteries and ley lines and history as we know it, publishes a fine newsletter called *Stonewatch.* If you are interested, write: Gungywamp Society, 36 Laurelwood Road, Groton, CT 06340.

Paul Devereux is one of the people spearheading the **Dragon Project** in England, whereby exacting measurements are being made of ley lines, energy leys, and grid work (energy patterns); also, magnetism studies are being done in and around ancient megalithic monuments. Paul is the author of four books on this subject: *Ley Hunter's Companion, Earth Lights, Lines on the Landscape: Leys and Other Enigmas* (with Nigel Pennick), and *Earthmind* (with John Steele and David Kubrin). He also publishes a magazine entitled, *The Ley Hunter: The Magazine of Earth Mysteries,* which is outstanding. Through Devereux, you can also obtain a very special and important book: *Games of the Gods: The Origin of Board Games in Magic and Divination,* by Nigel Pennick and published in England. Contact: Paul Devereux, P.O. Box 13, Welshpool, Powys, Wales, U.K. or P.O. Box 5, Brecon, Powys LD3 7AA, Wales, U.K.

The **Archaeological Conservancy** is an organization interested in buying sacred sites for the purpose of insuring their preservation. Considering the pace at which these sites are being torn down or destroyed, everyone's help is needed to stop the trend. Whether you have money to donate, ideas, or time to offer, contact them at 415 Orchard Drive, Santa Fe, NM 87501; phone (505) 982-3278.

William Becker and Bethe Hagens are two people who have done a great deal of work in researching and synthesizing maps and materials on earth grid lines and energy flows. Together they have produced the Earth Star polyhedron, a grid pattern of 120 identical triangles which our earth is supposedly moving toward in energy flows. If you are interested in learning more about earth energy, dowsing, geomancy, crystals, earth abnormalities, sacred geometry, astronomy, and ley lines, this subject is for you. The duo have made their work accessible to the general public through a set of materials you can buy. The set includes a cardboard fold-together model of Earth Star, a plastic overlay for the triangles, plus an article which explains what the polyhedron is all about. To obtain, write or call: Conservative Technology, 105 Wolpers Road, Park Forest, IL 60466; phone (312) 481-6168.

DOWSING

In Europe, dowsing is often referred to as **Baubiologie.** There is now in the United States an organization dedicated to the European approach to this subject which offers a correspondence course directed to those people who want to use dowsing to address hidden problems in their home, lands, businesses, or with their personal health. You may reach them through: International Institute for Baubiologie and Ecology, P.O. Box 387, Clearwater, FL 34615; phone (813) 461-4371.

The granddaddy of all dowsing organizations, however, and the least commercial, is **The American Society of Dowsers, Inc.** They are quite large, fully reputable, and sponsor a yearly conference each mid-September that is one of the finest events I have ever attended. Their digest is excellent, and they offer a full line of books, equipment, and materials related to the subject of dowsing. Many local chapters of the organization sprinkle the country, and regional conferences are held, as well. Write or call: The American Society of Dowsers, Danville, VT

05828-0024; phone (802) 684-3417.

Dowsing is the most constructive way I know to explore and expand intuitive/psychic abilities. And it is fun! Anyone from a four-year-old to a great-grandparent can do it. Contrary to some notions, dowsing is not a "special" gift but is readily teachable as a practical skill to access octaves of vibration beyond the electromagnetic spectrum. **Dowsers are the doers of PSI. The bottom line is always demonstration and results!** One of the best books written on the subject is:

The Divining Hand, by Christopher Bird. Black Mountain, NC; New Age Press, 1985.

GEOMANCY (FENG-SHUI)

Feng-Shui is **the art of living in harmony with the land** and deriving the greatest benefit, peace, and prosperity from being in the right place at the right time. It has two schools or systems of practice—the intuitive and the analytical—and in more recent times has been referred to as **Chinese geomancy.** Both easy and complicated, depending on which method you use, it is also immensely practical. It will help you build your home in proper balance with the land it sits upon, remodel what you already have into proper order, or assist you in planning rooms, decor, and usage of available space. Some helpful books on the subject are:

The Living Earth Manual of Feng-Shui, by Stephen Skinner. London, England; Routledge & Kegan Paul, 1982.

Feng Shui: The Chinese Art of Designing a Harmonious Environment, by Derek Walters. New York, NY; Simon & Schuster, 1988.

Feng Shui: The Chinese Art of Placement, by Sarah Rossbach. New York, NY; E.P. Dutton, 1983.

Interior Design With Feng Shui, by Sarah Rossbach. New York, NY; E.P. Dutton, 1987.

Feng-shui is helpful for restructuring what is already built by corresponding buildings to the earth's natural energy flow. This flow is called "dragon currents" or "chi" and compares favorably with east/west energy movements of the earth-pulse at about seven hertz. Geomancy utilizes north/south orientations to harness and redirect chi. Compasses were built to measure all aspects of this energy and assist with building construction. For this reason, feng-shui is the progenitor of modern magnetic compasses, navigation, and geography.

THE OLD WAYS

The word *pagan* simply means "country dweller" in Latin and refers to a more natural, harmonious way of living in accord with the rhythm of life as we know it on the earthplane. This particular viewpoint honors natural systems and cycles, the kingdoms of our little brothers and sisters (minerals, plants, animals), and the spirit keepers. It emphasizes intuition and sacredness. Here are some good references along this line of thinking:

> *The Way of the Shaman,* by Michael Harner. New York, NY; Bantam Books, 1982.

> *Spirit Song: The Visionary Wisdom of No-Eyes,* by Mary Summer Rain. Norfolk, VA; Donning Co., 1985.

> *Phoenix Rising: No-Eyes' Vision of the Changes to Come,* by Mary Summer Rain. Norfolk, VA; Donning Co., 1987.

> *Dreamwalker,* by Mary Summer Rain. Norfolk, VA; Donning Co., 1988.

> *Drawing Down the Moon,* by Margot Adler. New York, NY; Viking Press, 1979.

> *The Spiral Dance: A Rebirth of the Ancient Religion of the Great Goddess,* by Starhawk. New York, NY; Harper & Row, 1979.

> *Dreaming the Dark,* by Starhawk. Boston, MA; Beacon Press, 1982.

> *Magical Blend* magazine, P.O. Box 11303, San Francisco, CA 94101; phone (415) 282-9338.

> *Shaman's Drum* magazine, P.O. Box 16507, North Hollywood, CA 91615 (subscription service).

Wildfire magazine, previously mentioned, is a font of this kind of information, presented in a practical caring way. Other sources for learning the old ways are:

> *Center for Shamanic Studies,* Dance of the Deer Foundation,

P.O. Box 699, Soquel, CA 95073; phone (408) 475-9560.

The Foundation for Shamanic Studies, Box 670, Belden Station, Norwalk, CT 06852; phone (203) 454-2825.

Page Bryant Earth Studies Weekends, The Network for Cooperative Education, 130 Pinto Lane, Sedona, AZ 86336.

Twylah Nitsch (grandmother of The Wolf Clan of the Seneca Nation), 12199 Brant-Reservation Road, Irving, NY 14081; phone (716) 549-3889.

The Tracker Survival School, P.O. Box 173, Asbury, NJ 08802-0173; phone (201) 479-4681.

Circle Network News, Box 9013, Madison, WI 53715.

The Free Spirit Alliance, P.O. Box 5358, Laurel, MD 20707; phone (301) 445-0388.

Ecumenicon, 404 East Melbourne, Silver Spring, MD 20901.

DEVAS, NATURE SPIRITS, AND INTERSPECIES COMMUNICATION

Currently referred to as devas (shining ones) and nature spirits (spirit helpers), the angels and fairies of lore are making a comeback, mostly because so many diverse people in unrelated areas have had such remarkable experiences working with them. Most successful have been gardeners and those concerned with ecology. Legendary in this area of involvement is **the community of Findhorn,** located on the northeastern coast of Scotland. What began as an experiment to see how well humans could co-create with the spirit kingdoms in growing vegetables and flowers, became a show-place of spiritual law in action. Findhorn is extensive in scope. You can contact it directly for catalogues and information: The Accommodation Secretary, Findhorn Foundation, Cluny Hill College, Forres 1V36, ORD, Scotland; phone Forres (0309) 73655.

Some books on the subject of devas and nature spirits:

The Magic of Findhorn, by Paul Hawken. New York, NY; Harper & Row, 1975.

To Hear the Angels Sing: An Odyssey of Co-Creation With the Devic Kingdom, by Dorothy Maclean. Middletown, WI; Lorian Press, 1983.

Behaving as if the God in All Life Mattered and *The Perelandra Garden Workbook: A Complete Guide to Gardening with Nature Intelligences*, both by Machaelle Small Wright. Available through Perelandra, Ltd., Box 136, Jeffersonton, VA 22724.

Animal Dreaming was written by Jim Nollman after fifteen years of researching human/animal communications with species as varied as whales, mosquitoes, turkeys, and buffalo. Originally published in Great Britain as *Dolphin Dreamtime*, the book was brought to the United States in 1987 through Bantam Books. Public response to *Animal Dreaming* enabled Nollman to initiate a non-profit, educational organization called **Interspecies Communications**, which offers a host of services in its effort to preserve the environment and to respect the consciousness and wisdom of animals. By combining art with science, a number of musical projects have also ensued. Membership is annual. Write: Interspecies Communication, 273 Hidden Meadow Lane, Friday Harbor, WA 98250. Nollman's latest book is *Spiritual Ecology*, published by Bantam Books in 1990.

Outstanding books on the subject of **interspecies communication** are:

Kinship With All Life, by J. Allen Boone. New York, NY; Harper & Row, 1976.

Talking with Nature, by Michael J. Roads. Tiburon, CA; H.J. Kramer, Inc., 1987.

The Human/Animal Connection, edited by Randall L. Eaton. Crystal Bay, NV; Carnivore Press, 1985.

Animal Thinking, by Donald Griffin. Cambridge, MA; Harvard University Press, 1984.

The Immortal Wilderness, by John Hay. New York, NY; W. W. Norton & Co., 1987.

Walk When the Moon Is Full, by Frances Hamerstrom (for children of all ages). Trumansburg, NY; Crossing Press, 1975.

Who Speaks for Wolf, by Paula Underwood Spencer. Available from Tribe of Two Press, P.O. Box 1763, Austin, TX 78767. By the time you read this, *Who Speaks for Wolf* may be out of print from Tribe of Two Press, but contact them anyway for they will have information on where to obtain it and what other writings have been published by Paula Underwood Spencer. Spencer, by the way, is one of the finest Native American writers publishing today, and I recommend her work highly.

DREAMS & MYTHOLOGY

How to Interpret Your Own Dreams: An Encyclopedic Dictionary, by Tom Chetwynd. New York, NY; P.H. Wyden, 1980.

The Dream Dictionary, by Jo Jean Boushahla and Virginia Reidel-Geubtner. New York, NY; Pilgrim, 1983.

Lucid Dreaming: The Power of Being Awake and Aware in Your Dreams, by Stephen LaBerge, Ph.D. Los Angeles, CA; J.P. Tarcher, 1985.

The Inner Eye: Your Dreams Can Make You Psychic, by Joan Windsor. Englewood Cliffs, NJ; Prentice-Hall, 1985.

Personal Mythology: The Psychology of Your Evolving Self: Using Ritual, Dreams, and Imagination to Discover Your Inner Story, by David Feinstein, Ph.D. and Stanley Krippner, Ph.D. Los Angeles, CA; J.P. Tarcher, 1988.

Three incredible thinkers have produced **important works on the subjects of mythology, and sacred and secret mysteries.** They are:

The Secret Teachings of All Ages, by Manly P. Hall. Originally published in 1928 by the Philosophical Research Society of Los Angeles, CA. Reprinted in 1978.

The Power of Myth, by Joseph Campbell with Bill Moyers. New York, NY; Doubleday, 1988. This book is a summary of the PBS television series. Moyers interviewed Campbell, the world's foremost authority on myths, on the power and purpose of mythology. The series was so compelling that it also became six one-hour video and audio programs. This series should be available through any bookstore, or you can order it from Mystic Fire Video, P.O. Box 30969, New York, NY 10011; phone 1-800-727-8433.

Memories and Visions of Paradise: Exploring the Universal Myth of a Lost Golden Age, by Richard Heinberg. Los Angeles, CA; J.P. Tarcher, 1989.

INTUITION AND THE PSYCHIC

Logic and intuition are equal partners. Without both working together harmoniously, we are neither healthy nor balanced. Logic, a product of conscious and deliberate thought, is considered a left-brain activity. Intuition, a product of subconscious abstractions, is most often associated with the right hemisphere of the brain. There has been ample scientific research now to prove the wisdom of **right-brain development** and the folly of exclusive dependence on left-brain linear thinking. A healthy brain is a whole brain, in which all parts work together effectively and equally.

As we expand our creative and intuitive potential, we develop solid, dependable skills and abilities with which to explore our inner life and dreamscapes. A question to ask is: How can we ever reach and endure transcended states of consciousness until we can first learn to utilize and integrate the inner realities of our own mind? Visualization and dream interpretation are positive, safe ways to begin.

The dynamics of inner realities are really the same thing as psychic abilities. The only difference is one of semantics. **The psychic and the intuitive are the same!** Psychic powers are simply extensions of natural sensing faculties normal to us. It is all a matter of usage and purpose. Perhaps the best way to think of this and keep everything in a healthy perspective is to concentrate on developing ourselves to be the best we can, to emphasize virtue, responsibility, joy, and service. All else will assume its rightful proportions if we do.

Psychic ability developed just for the sake of being psychic boomerangs.

Forgive me if I seem to be repeating myself here, but this issue is so important. Notice, for instance, how many psychics lead miserable lives and/or drink excessively, smoke heavily, or are hooked on drugs and sex. **Being "accurate" is not necessarily a sign of competence.** Psychic abilities developed out of context from our practical and spiritual natures represents the negative aspect of inner growth, in my opinion. But, psychic abilities developed as part of a balanced, wholesome life are invaluable. Skills of the inner life are just as valid and desirable as skills of the outer life. And, anything you can already do you can always learn to do better!

The best established organization, which serves as a guidepost for the sane, constructive exploration of psychism as it relates to wholesome, spiritual development, is the **Association for Research and Enlightenment** (A.R.E.). Highly diversified, they offer a complete range of books, tapes, class and seminar opportunities, therapeutic departments, a health clinic, a list of cooperating doctors, summer camps, study groups throughout the world, library facilities, Atlantic University for the study of consciousness, ongoing research projects, and much, much more. Their magazine, *Venture Inward,* is the best in its field. Introductory packets with book catalogue are free for the asking. Contact: A.R.E., P.O. Box 595, Virginia Beach, VA 23451; phone (804) 428-3588. They are located on the corner of 67th and Atlantic Avenue in Virginia Beach. Their programs for beginners are especially good.

Another reliable organization, which is more of a movement than a fixed-base operation, is **Spiritual Frontiers Fellowship** (S.F.F.). Although not as large as A.R.E., and not offering the same programs for beginners, they do have a challenging and very stimulating summertime seminar program at various college campuses across the country. Attracting some of the finest talent in the field, their seminars are lively and enjoyable as well as diverse. Their quarterly journal is excellent. S.F.F. also maintains a library, local study groups, and various educational programs. Queries are welcome. Their new address is: S.F.F., P.O. Box 7868, Philadelphia, PA 19101.

Although not as large or diverse as the two previous organizations, **Spiritual Advisory Council** (S.A.C.) deserves to be mentioned. In existence for over fifteen years, the organization has established itself as a source of outstanding summertime seminars held in various locations, plus classes and ministerial programs for the purpose of teaching the spiritual use of psychic abilities. National and international speakers are often featured. Queries welcome. Contact: Spiritual Advisory Council, 2965 W. State Road 434, Suite 300, Longwood, FL 32779; phone (305) 774-6151.

Two of the most constructive and practical manuals for psychic development are not available in bookstores as of this writing. Contact directly:

Harold Sherman's Great ESP Manual, Mrs. Harold Sherman, Highway South, Mountain View, AR 72560

Practical ESP: A Step by Step Guide for Developing Your Intuitive Potential, Carol Ann Liaros, Blind Awareness Project, 1966 Niagara Street, Suite 101, Buffalo, NY 14207.

To broaden your understanding of this field, try:

The Mind Race: Understanding and Using Psychic Abilities, by Russell Targ and Keith Harary. New York, NY; Ballantine, 1985.

Venture Inward, by Hugh Lynn Cayce. New York, NY; Harper & Row, 1985.

Stalking the Wild Pendulum: On the Mechanics of Consciousness, by Itzhak Bentov. New York, NY; E.P. Dutton, 1977.

A Cosmic Book: On the Mechanics of Creation, by Itzhak Bentov and Mirtala. New York, NY; E.P. Dutton, 1982.

Videos: "Mandalas: Vision of Heaven and Earth" and "The Human Journey" both feature the transformational sculpture and poetry of Mirtala set to music. Order from Mirtala, P.O. Box 465, Belmont, MA 02178.

Corinne McLaughlin of the Sirius Community in Shutesbury, MA, has produced an excellent small booklet entitled, *How to Evaluate Psychic Guidance and Channeling*. It is inexpensive and highly recommended. Write: Sirius Publishing, Sirius Community, Baker Road, Shutesbury, MA 01072; phone (413) 259-1505.

The Center for Applied Intuition was founded in 1979 and exists to help people develop, refine, and control their intuitive abilities so they can more effectively apply them to the practical demands of a busy and increasingly complex world. The Center is set up to assist scientists in developing new research angles, help executives make clear decisions, and enable individuals to help executives make clear decisions, and enable individuals to feel more in tune and at peace in their daily lives. A membership newsletter is available. For more information, write or call: Center for Applied Intuition, 2046 Clement Street, San Francisco, CA 94121; phone (415) 221-1280.

Rabbit Writer's Project: Kids Helping Kids Newsletter is especially designed for youngsters exploring their own natural abilities. It takes them on a magic-flying-carpet ride through realms of imagination and creativity. Any child can participate. Inquire: A Rabbit Writer's Project, P.O. Box 143, Dania, FL 33004.

A reputable psychic reader functions like a mirror, reflecting back to you what you put out, and like a flashlight, helping you to see your path more clearly. His or her job is to provide information and insight—nothing more. As in any other facet of life, don't believe everything you hear and always seek another opinion. Here are three top publications:

Body, Mind and Spirit magazine, P.O. Box 701, Providence, RI 02901.

Fate magazine, P.O. Box 249, Highland Park, IL 60035.

Woodrew Update Newsletter, 448 Rabbit Skin Road, Waynesville, NC 28786. Greta Woodrew's latest book, *Memories of Tomorrow,* was published in 1988 by Dolphin Books, a division of Doubleday in New York. Although diverse and well-grounded, Greta also channels material from extraterrestrials.

SPIRITUALITY AND MEDITATION

Meditation is a helpful way to facilitate and maintain the inner journey based on commitment and discipline. It is not some brand name sold upon an open market of pie-in-the-sky promises. There is no quick high to be had and no one has a monopoly on the subject. Meditative life consists of phases and cycles as the process assists you with inner cleansing and inner purification. It changes as you change, yet it always offers the steadiness of spiritual growth. There are many methods and countless styles. One of my favorite teachers is the practical and humorous **Eknath Easwaran**. His book and album, *Meditation: Commonsense Directions for an Uncommon Life,* are excellent. Founder of the Blue Mountain Center for Meditation and a successful college professor, Easwaran has written many books, all available through: Nilgiri Press, Box 477, Petaluma, CA 94953; phone (707) 878-2369.

Some other books on **meditation** and its complement, **affirmative prayer,** are:

> *An Easy Guide to Meditation,* by Roy Eugene Davis. Available from CSA Press, P.O. Box 7, Lake Rabun Road, Lakemont, GA 30552.

> *How to Meditate,* by Lawrence LeShan. New York, NY; Bantam Books, 1975.

> *The Miracle of Mindfulness: A Manual on Meditation,* by Thich Nhat Hanh. Boston, MA; Beacon Press, 1976.

> *The Chakras,* by C.W. Leadbeater. Wheaton, IL; Knowledge Systems, Inc., 1988.

> *Chakras: Energy Centers of Transformation,* by Harish Johari. Rochester, VT; Destiny Books, 1987.

> *Energy, Ecstasy, and Your Seven Vital Chakras,* by Bernard Gunther. North Hollywood, CA; Newcastle, 1983.

> *My Magic Garden,* by Ilse Klipper (a meditation guide for children). Available from Science of Mind Publications, P.O. Box 75127, Los Angeles, CA 90075.

> *Receptive Prayer* and *A Manual of Receptive Prayer,* both by Grace Adolphsen Brame. Available from Science of Mind Publications, P.O. Box 75127, Los Angeles, CA 90075.

> *The Dynamic Laws of Prayer,* by Catherine Ponder. Available from DeVorss & Company, P.O. Box 550, Marina Del Rey, CA 90294.

Spirituality is based upon a personal, intimate experience of God. There are no standards or dogmas, only precedents, for individual knowing or gnosis is honored. Because it is so personal, methodologies are often elusive or confusing at best. So here is a caution to remember: **There is no system of spiritual**

enlightenment that can guarantee spiritual attainment. Just because someone thinks he or she is spiritual doesn't mean that person is. Always look to the results, the consequences, for after-effects cannot be faked. My own personal yardstick says, "If you can't live what you know to be true, then it isn't worth knowing."

The spiritual path is truly "The Inner Journey," deep within the depths of your inner self, and it entails a thorough "house cleaning" on every level of your being. The challenge is to find the God within and reconnect, and that means a lifetime commitment. Spirituality is a lifestyle, as well as a philosophic belief and inner knowing.

Some excellent books **which illumine the spiritual perspective** are:

Practical Mysticism, by Evelyn Underhill. Available from Ariel Press, P.O. Box 30975, Columbus, OH 43230.

Western Spirituality: Historical Roots, Ecumenical Routes, by Matthew Fox. Santa Fe, NM; Bear & Company, 1987.

The Problem Is God: The Selection and Care of Your Personal God, by C. Alan Anderson, Ph.D. Walpole, NH; Stillpoint Press, 1984. Anderson also wrote *God in a Nutshell* and *Metaphysical Mousetraps,* both excellent and available from Three Arches Bookstore, P.O. Box 75127, Los Angeles, CA 90075.

The Road Less Traveled: A New Psychology of Love, Traditional Values and Spiritual Growth, by M. Scott Peck, M.D. New York, NY; Simon & Schuster, 1980.

Ordinary People as Monks and Mystics: Lifestyles for Self-Discovery, by Marsha Sinetar. Mahwah, NJ; Paulist Press, 1986.

Do What You Love, the Money Will Follow: Discovering Your Right Livelihood, by Marsha Sinetar. Mahwah, NJ; Paulist Press, 1987.

Being Peace, by Thich Nhat Hanh. Berkeley, CA; Parallax Press, 1987.

The Travelling People's Feild Guide, by Reshad Feild. New York, NY; Element Books, 1986.

The Immense Journey, by Loren Eiseley. New York, NY;
Random House, 1957.

The Re-Enchantment of the World, by Morris Berman.
Ithaca, NY; Cornell University Press, 1981.

Magic at Our Hand, by Nancy Rose Exeter. Available from
Emissary Foundation International, 4817 North County
Road 29, Loveland, CO 80537.

When You Can Walk on Water, Take the Boat, by John Har-
richaran. Marietta, GA; New World Publishing, 1988.

The New Age, by David Spangler. Issaquah, WA; Morning-
town, Inc., 1988.

Discovering Your Soul's Purpose, by Mark Thurston. Available as a study kit from A.R.E. Bookstore, P.O. Box 595,
Virginia Beach, VA 23451.

The Prophet, by Kahlil Gibran. New York, NY; Alfred A.
Knopf, in continuous printings—a timeless classic.

*Sacred Sites: A Traveler's Guide to North America's Most
Powerful, Mystical Landmarks,* by Natasha Peterson.
Chicago, IL; Contemporary Books, 1988.

Science of Mind magazine, with the daily guides to richer
living. Contact: Science of Mind Magazine, P.O. Box
75127, Los Angeles, CA 90075.

Good books on **reincarnation** are:

Eye of the Centaur, by Barbara Hand Clow. St. Paul, MN;
Llewellyn Publications, 1986.

The Journey Within, by Henry Leo Bolduc. Virginia Beach,
VA; Inner Vision, 1988.

The Search for Omm Sety: Reincarnation and Eternal Love,
by Jonathan Cott. Garden City, NY; Doubleday & Co.,
1987.

Many Lives, Many Masters, by Brian Weiss, M.D. New York,
NY; Simon & Schuster, 1988.

The Mountains of Tibet, by Mordicai Gerstein. New York,
NY; Harper's Junior Books, 1987. This is the best book, by
the way, I have yet found on the subject for children.

Special books on **life and death for children** are:

The Hour Glass: Sixty Fables for This Moment in Time, by Carl Japikse. Ariel, OH; Ariel Press, 1984.

Hope for the Flowers, by Trina Paulus. New York, NY; Paulist Press, 1972.

The Fall of Freddie the Leaf, by Leo Buscaglia, Ph.D. Thorofare, NJ; Charles G. Slack, Inc., 1982.

You—A Source of Strength in Our World, by Eleanor Rost (especially good for grade school ages). Available from Coleman Publishing, 99 Milbar Blvd., Farmingdale, NY 11735.

Animalia, by Barbara Berger. Berkeley, CA; Celestial Arts, 1982.

When the Sun Rose, by Barbara Berger. New York, NY; Putnam Publishing Group, 1986.

Grandfather Twilight, by Barbara Berger. New York, NY; Putnam Publishing Group, 1986.

Who Speaks for Wolf, by Paula Underwood Spencer. Available from Tribe of Two Press, P.O. Box 1763, Austin, TX 78767.

The Door to the Secret City and a cassette dramatization of the book (same name), both by Kathleen J. Forti. This special set depicts the near-death experience from a child's view. Available from: Kids Want Answers, Too!, P.O. Box 297, Virginia Beach, VA 23458; phone (804) 422-2925.

A Course in Miracles is an in-depth guide to spiritual development, and it has inspired millions to make significant changes for the better in their lives. Available as a three-volume set or as a single edition, it can be purchased through most bookstores or from Inner Peace, P.O. Box 635, Tiburon, CA 94920. Additional and complimentary materials can be obtained from: **Miracle Distribution Center,** 1141 East Ash Avenue, Fullerton, CA 92631; phone (714) 738-8380; and **Foundation for a Course in Miracles,** P.O. Box 783, Crompond, NY 10517-0783; phone (914) 528-0101.

ELISABETH KÜBLER-ROSS CENTER

I know of no one who has done so much for so many as Elisabeth Kübler-Ross, M.D. Her methods for releasing pain and fear, and developing a more loving and grounded lifestyle, are incredible. Her books are classics. Her work with dying patients is legendary. But her best work, in my opinion, are the week-long, intensive, live-in workshops she has established. Although famous for work with death and dying, Elisabeth is now dedicated to the upliftment of life and the practice of unconditional love. To become a member of her Center or inquire about the workshops and materials, contact: The Elisabeth Kübler-Ross Center, South Route #616, Head Waters, VA 24442; phone (703) 396-3441.

NEAR-DEATH EXPERIENCE

For more information about the near-death experience, contact the **International Association for Near-Death Studies, Inc.,** P.O. Box 7767, Philadelphia, PA 19101-7767. They have several brochures to offer, education and referral services, journal and newsletter publications, plus a list of books written on the subject. Queries are always welcome.

By P.M.H. Atwater:

Coming Back to Life: The After-Effects of the Near-Death Experience. Hardcover Dodd, Mead & Company, NY, 1988. Paperback Ballantine Books, NY, 1989.

The After-Effects: The Untold Story of the Near-Death Experience in video format, VHS or BETA. This video and a line of self-help audio tapes are available from: YOU CAN Change Your Life, P.O. Box 7691, Charlottesville, VA 22906.

Always look beyond
what you can see,
for the purpose
of truth
is
to extend
your view.

Thank you
for reading
this book.

I hope it has
brought you joy.

about
the author

Born in Twin Falls, Idaho, P.M.H. Atwater married young and became a wife, mother, Sunday School teacher, secretary, and prize-winning cook. In the mid-sixties, she received a handwriting analysis which revealed talents she did not know she had. This prompted a complete career change into the specialties of projects development, public service, business analysis, and promotions. She paralleled her career change with intense studies of altered states of consciousness and spirituality. This led to professional work in the fields of hypnotic past-life regression, dehaunting houses, sensitivity, astrology, numerology, dream and symbol interpretation, earth energies, and divination. Her biography appears in sixteen *Who's Who* volumes, half of them international editions.

In 1977, severe medical problems set the stage for Atwater to have three near-death experiences within a span of three months. After she had recovered her health, she walked out on her life and on everything she had known to follow a new vision. She began to seek out others like herself who had had near-death experiences, and launched a study which resulted in the book, *Coming Back to Life: The After-Effects of the Near-Death Experience*. This is the first book of a three-part series. Book two is titled *Future Memory: A Journey Through Alternate Realities and the Illusion of Time and Space*.

Rune casting came into Atwater's life in 1978, just before she left Idaho. The rune-casting process became invaluable to her as a way to balance intellect with intuition, the head with the heart. Writing *The Magical Language of Runes* was a chance for her to pass along the wonders of spirit to others.

Married twice, the mother of three and grandmother of one, Atwater has now committed herself to redefining health and the fullness of life.

Another book by the author:

Coming Back to Life:
The After-Effects of the Near-Death Experience

BOOKS OF RELATED INTEREST
BY BEAR & COMPANY

MEDICINE CARDS
The Discovery of Power
Through the Ways of Animals
by Jamie Sams & David Carson

AT THE POOL OF WONDER
Dreams & Visions of an Awakening Humanity
by Marcia Lauck & Deborah Koff-Chapin

HEART OF THE CHRISTOS
Starseeding from the Pleiades
by Barbara Hand Clow

THE EMERGING NEW AGE
by J. L. Simmons

SECRETS OF MAYAN SCIENCE/RELIGION
by Hunbatz Men

SACRED PLACES IN NATURE
How the Living Earth Seeks Our Friendship
by James Swan

Contact your local bookseller or write:
BEAR & COMPANY
P.O. Drawer 2860
Santa Fe, NM 87504